Freedom from the Prison of Addiction

Spiritual and Secular Wisdom

Martina Killeavy

Contents

Preface by Greg Boyle SJ 5

Introduction.. 7

What Are the Spiritual Exercises? 14

What Is the Twelve-Step Programme?.. 15

Preparation and Prayer before Each Reflection 16

Reflection 1: St Ignatius and the Spiritual Exercises.................. 19

Reflection 2: Your Image of God 25

Reflection 3: The Negative Forces of Sin in the World.............. 31

Reflection 4: Despite My Sinfulness, I Am Loved by God 40

Reflection 5: God's Mercy and Healing 48

Reflection 6: Love of God and Love of Self................................ 53

Reflection 7: The Passion and Death of Jesus............................ 61

Reflection 8: The Call of the King... 67

Reflection 9: Saying Yes to God: The Response of Mary 75

Reflection 10: Temptations.. 80

Reflection 11: The Resurrection of Jesus.................................... 88

Reflection 12: So, What Do YOU Want? 92

Afterword by Peter McVerry SJ 100

Appendix One: Summary of Reflections.................................... 105

Appendix Two: The Way of the Cross: A Prison
Perspective, Led by Pope Francis, Good Friday 2020................ 109

About Dialogue for Diversity and the Jesuit
Centre for Faith and Justice... 128

Preface by Greg Boyle SJ

The prophet Ezekiel writes, 'The spirit entered me and set me on my feet'. Part of the human experience is to be laid low, flat on our face, occasionally, and in need of being lifted up. The point of being 'set on our feet' is not just to stand but to walk. Our aim is to walk each other home to wholeness and to find our utter fullness in the God who loves us without measure and without regret.

Martina Killeavy's reflections and guidance here sets us on our feet. The marriage of the Twelve-Step principles to the dynamism of Ignatian spirituality is enormously helpful and a breakthrough in our common quest for wellness and relational wholeness.

It has been the privilege of my life to have my heart altered for these past thirty-seven years by thousands of gang members in Los Angeles. 15,000 folks a year walk through our doors at Homeboy Industries, the largest gang-intervention, rehab and recovery program on the planet. They find welcome, safety to re-direct their lives and a graced opportunity to discover the truth of who they are: exactly what God had in mind, when God made them. 'Oh nobly born,' the Buddhists say, 'remember who you really are.'

The other day, I was trying to convince a young homie to begin his journey of recovery. I tried to nudge him towards one of our various Twelve-Step groups. 'AA doesn't work', he insisted. Of course, every-one knows the answer to that. 'It works, if you work it.'

Martina's reflections suggest a practice, soaked with a depth of God's own spaciousness and a keen knowledge of the Spiritual Exercises, that each of us can embrace each day. This 'practice' doesn't make 'perfect' but establishes a pattern of gratitude, an affinity to stay anchored in the present moment and a facility to find God in all things. The practice of these reflections and steps helps us find room in our hearts for each other as we 'walk home' together. The passage-way presented here is a guide to finding our true selves in loving. Exactly what God had in mind. The joy of this path is knowing that what we most deeply want IS what God wants for us. And yes, it works if you work it.

Above all, these reflections aid the participant in locating the God we actually have and not the partial God we've settled for. Ignatius knew the God of love, and as Mirabai Starr writes, 'Once you know the God of love, you fire all the other gods.' The God presented here, the one Ignatius knew, is expansive, compassionate and tender. We feel ourselves receiving the tenderness of God and find the compelling invitation to become that tenderness in the world. We can then freely choose, through this practice, to be in the world as God wants us to be.

We begin here to be 'set on our feet' and can do no other than love being loving. We find God's dream come true in creating and fostering a community of kinship such that God might recognise. We choose, in freedom, to cherish with every breath we take and, as Ignatius would say, 'relish' what is right in front of us. These reflections help us to go where love has not yet arrived and love what we find there. And the circle of compassion is widened so that no one is standing outside of it.

Martina directs us all to apply the genius of Ignatius to our ordinary lives. She leads us to the mystical vision of seeing God as 'the Pilgrim' did: 'The God who is always greater.' O nobly born. The gift of this journey is to inhabit our shared dignity and nobility. And with Ignatius of Loyola we can 'take care, to keep always before our eyes ... first ... God'.

Greg Boyle SJ is Director of Homeboy Industries, Los Angeles

Introduction

An alcoholic once told me that when you hit rock bottom there is only one way left to go, and that's up. I'm not sure I agreed with him. He was lucky that he made it but many don't.

My first encounter with alcohol abuse was when I was a very young child, about seven years old. We lived in a beautiful part of Munster, in the south of Ireland. Behind our house there were green fields and mountains where the heather bloomed throughout the summer, and it was magical to look out at it. As children, we would go up the mountain road for a walk, pick wild flowers and make necklaces with the buttercups and daisies that grew in the fields.

When we got to the top of the mountain there was a valley with a few houses scattered around and a small lagoon. In the summer many of the locals who had emigrated to England and America during the 1940s and 1950s would come home on holidays, and they would walk the mountain path to inhale the fresh air and take in the beauty that surrounded them.

Up that same mountain road lived a few families, most of them very poor, with just a goat grazing to provide some sustenance. Every so often, after midnight, when we children would be fast asleep at night in bed, a little girl called Sheila (not her real name), who lived up the mountain, would come knocking on our door crying for help. I would be awakened with her crying and banging on the front door. My father would get up and go off with her.

Then there would be silence.

It was very dark as there were no street lights up that lonely mountain road, just the light of the moon if you were lucky. I would lie awake for a while, wondering what was wrong. Then I would hear my father return, and I would know that all was well again and go back to sleep.

The next morning at breakfast nothing would be said, but one morning after one of these episodes, I heard my father whispering to my mother that Sheila's father came home drunk again and started to beat them up.

Sheila wouldn't be at school that day. She would be marked out sick. When she did come back, she would sit in her seat and stare at me. I can still see her face. It was pale and drawn. She had short, dark hair and glacial green eyes, but her face was serious and lifeless. She never smiled. We never spoke. Just two young kids looking silently at each other and both knowing at some level that things were not right.

I have often wondered since what she was thinking. She probably thought that I was one of the lucky children, something I wasn't aware of at the time. Neither was I aware of what she was going through. She dropped out of school soon after. I never saw her again, but I never forgot her sad face.

At school today there are children in classes all over the country, learning and singing and being happy. But there are at least one or two just sitting there staring around the room with cold eyes. They say nothing because the night before they were shaken to pieces listening to their parents calling each other names, throwing the dinner at the wall, breaking the furniture and beating them if they cried, while their father or mother, or both, acted out their drunken rage. This is happening every night in our towns and cities. Most of it does not come to the ears of social services.

Children do not get over these experiences easily. Unfortunately, some follow the same path when they become adults because they want to numb their pain, and the only way that they have learned to do this is with drink or drugs.

The level of alcohol and drug abuse in our society is frightening.

In my work as a counselling psychologist, I saw that addiction was much broader than alcohol, drugs and tobacco. It also includes addiction to gambling, the internet, pornography, shopping, social media, power, money and sex.

Many have argued that the use of alcohol and illegal drugs is a means to achieve a transcendent state of consciousness. They conclude that addiction is related to an unfulfilled spirituality, a thirst for unity with the spiritual self. I tend to agree. In my own work, I found that those who use Alcoholics Anonymous (AA) and similar groups, and who can put their trust in a higher power, whatever that may be for them, have a much better recovery rate than those who think they can go it alone.

Swiss psychiatrist Carl Jung believed that the craving for alcohol was really a craving for wholeness, a union with a higher force he called God. He described alcoholism as a spiritual disease and suggested that the way to overcome it was by a spiritual awakening. Through such an awakening, people can get in touch with what is really important to them at their deepest level.

Bill Wilson, co-founder of AA, also considered the excessive use of alcohol to be a search for a higher consciousness and concluded that the conversion experience involves a deep collapse of our false egos. When our ego is out of kilter, we exaggerate our self-importance. At the same time, we feel deeply inferior to others, and we mask this by pretending that we are full of confidence. What AA members refer to as 'hitting rock bottom' is a surrendering of this false ego. This leads to the beginning of humility, honesty and openness. This is similar to what many saints found in their own conversion journey, not least Ignatius who gave us the Spiritual Exercises.

Addiction not only affects the addict, but at least ten others among family and friends. Alcoholism is an infectious disease, just like Covid-19, and over the centuries it has killed hundreds of thousands more than the number killed by Covid-19 in Ireland. The devastation that alcohol and drug abuse bring to people's lives and on their families and friends is heartbreaking.

Addiction is no respecter of classes. In fact it is a great leveller of economic difference. The rich, however, have easier access to treatment. As it happens, most of my engagement has been with working-class people, more women than men, and prisoners, both pre- and post-release. In this book, I outline a series of reflections that I developed over the years with others and helped to guide. The vast majority who took part in them found them helpful. This does not mean that all were freed from addiction, but I hope that by taking part in them, they were supported and encouraged on their journey. When people find freedom it is always because of a change that comes from inside them. That change is mysterious. I believe that it can be helped by people other than the addict, but only when the addict is ready: when that mysterious movement of grace has begun within them.

So, when I think of alcohol and drug abuse:

- I think of all the children in school today who will go home to a drunken parent or one addicted to other drugs lying on the couch in a catatonic state.
- I think of the millions of children around the world who will face sexual abuse tonight because of an alcohol- or drug-abusing parent.
- I think of all the children who will go without food tonight because the money has been spent on alcohol and/or other drugs.
- I think of all the women and men who will be beaten up tonight or raped because their partners are addicted to alcohol or other drugs.
- I think of the person next on the list to get murdered because the drug addict can't pay the dealer for his or her drugs.
- I think of the next car accident caused by a drunken driver who is going to leave someone dead and a family shattered for years to come.
- I think of all the people whose lives have been irrevocably damaged because of the abuse of alcohol and other drugs, which led to everyday muggings, robberies and other crimes, often carried out on the most vulnerable in our society, like the elderly.
- I think of all those young people who have ended up in prison because of what alcohol and other drugs did to them before they had the wit to walk away.
- I think of the drug dealers and find it hard to find mercy for them because of the devastation they cause. If I knew their story, however, I might find that they were dealing with their own pain.

These associations are very different from those that addicts have with alcohol and other drugs. Instead they connect them with pleasure. When they are drunk or stoned, they feel good, chilled out and relaxed. While the alcohol and other drugs may do this at first, the more they take, the more they build up their tolerance, and the more they need to reach a high. Then they are hooked.

We learn our associations with alcohol and other drugs, good or bad, in our families, from our culture and especially from advertising. Too often drinking is seen as cool. It is paired with popularity and being sociable, with finding happiness and friendship. If children are hurt, lonely, abused or neglected while growing up, marketing will tell them that they can find a way out of their pain. Eventually, for far too many, addiction leads to losing jobs, marriage, children, health, self-respect and integrity, or ending up in prison for things they never wanted to do in the first place.

We are born into a culture that encourages alcohol drinking, which for many is the gateway to other drugs. Alcohol is framed positively in the Irish psyche. We talk about it as if it is embedded in our cultural DNA, not just acceptable but almost integral.

Some years ago I trained in Spiritual Direction. As part of this process, I completed the Spiritual Exercises of Ignatius and realised this process put me in touch with a deeper part of myself. In my work with people in addiction, I could see a close connection between the Spiritual Exercises and the Twelve-Step Programme of AA.

I also became more aware of the limitations of psychology. Psychology plays an important role in helping us understand the journey that those struggling with addiction and abuse are on. Moreover, it helps us understand our own journeys in life. I have come to believe, however, that more is needed. I have found that healing only comes when people touch into a deeper, spiritual part of themselves. In my experience, this is especially true of those dealing with addiction and abuse.

In recent years, I volunteered to work in one of our prisons. There I met hundreds of prisoners, many of them young. Most were there because of alcohol and other drugs, which had led to their criminal behaviour. This included robbery, assaults and break-ins to get money to feed their addiction. Some were there for murder, domestic violence and sexual abuse, most of which were carried out under the influence of both alcohol and other drugs. Many left broken relationships and lost children outside. Some were highly competent people who found themselves in this situation because the alcohol and other drugs had taken complete control of their lives. This often happened as a response to the pain they felt from abuse, broken homes, depression, anxiety, post-traumatic stress, attention deficit disorder and other illnesses.

With others, I shared a series of reflections that introduced participants – most of whom had problems with addiction – to elements of the Spiritual Exercises. All our sessions included questions for participants to reflect on. We made clear that the questions and answers were between themselves and God, so there was no sharing in the group. The advantage of this was that it reduced the pressure on people to come up with answers that they thought might impress others, and also avoided the danger of one individual dominating the group.

This book is an expansion of these reflections and is aimed at anyone struggling with addiction and those who care for them. Some reflections are longer than others and these can be spread over a few sessions. This is not a book to be read in one sweep like a novel. Each reflection should take time and space.

The reflections are written as simply as possible so that they are accessible to those with little formal education or knowledge of the Scriptures. There is some repetition for two reasons. Firstly, it takes time for ideas to sink in. Secondly, Ignatius in the Exercises frequently stresses the need for repetition.

These reflections are not an attempt to give the full Spiritual Exercises but rather some elements of them, especially from the First Week.

Addiction is widespread in our society. Children as young as thirteen are being admitted to hospitals for overdoses. Anyone who has been to our A&E departments knows the reality of addiction. When people think of addiction, they often think of drug addiction first and foremost. Many of the people I meet don't see alcohol as a drug, and yet alcohol can be as destructive as any other drug. The main focus of this book is on addiction to alcohol and other drugs, but the reflections that follow can also be applied to many other forms of addiction: pornography, gambling, the internet, wealth, work, and power.

Struggling against addiction is incredibly difficult. My hope is that the reflections in this book may help some overcome their demons.

Martina Killeavy, 1 January 2023

What Are the Spiritual Exercises?

The Spiritual Exercises are meditations, prayers and spiritual practices developed by Ignatius in the sixteenth century. These meditations, prayers and spiritual practices were written down by St Ignatius in a book called *The Spiritual Exercises* from 1522–1524. The Exercises are very important to the Society of Jesus (the Jesuits), which Ignatius founded. Today, the Exercises are made accessible to people through a variety of retreats and programmes. You can learn more about the Exercises here: https://www.manresa.ie/ignatian-spirituality/the -spiritual-exercises.

What Is the Twelve-Step Programme?

The Twelve-Step Programme of AA is based on a programme originally outlined in Bill Wilson's book *Alcoholics Anonymous: The Story of How More than One Hundred Men Have Recovered from Alcoholism* published in 1939. It was collaboratively written by those involved in early AA groups established by Bill Wilson and Bob Smith. Over decades, the Twelve-Step Programme has been adapted to address all kinds of addiction and has helpted millions. I will adapt the original twelve steps as necessary throughout this book. The original twelve steps are:

1. We admitted we were powerless over alcohol – that our lives had become unmanageable.
2. Came to believe that a power greater than ourselves could restore us to sanity.
3. Made a decision to turn our will and our lives over to the care of God *as we understood him.*
4. Made a searching and fearless moral inventory of ourselves.
5. Admitted to God, to ourselves, and to another human being the exact nature of our wrongs.
6. Were entirely ready to have God remove all these defects of character.
7. Humbly asked him to remove our shortcomings.
8. Made a list of all persons we had harmed, and became willing to make amends to them all.
9. Made direct amends to such people wherever possible, except when to do so would injure them or others.
10. Continued to take personal inventory, and when we were wrong, promptly admitted it.
11. Sought through prayer and meditation to improve our conscious contact with God *as we understood him*, praying only for knowledge of his will for us and the power to carry that out.
12. Having had a spiritual awakening as the result of these steps, we tried to carry this message to alcoholics and to practise these principles in all our affairs.

Preparation and Prayer before Each Reflection

Before beginning any reflection, it is always helpful to take a few moments to quieten down and find some stillness within yourself. Becoming quiet is necessary to allow the mind to be still and listen to God. You need to become conscious that you are entering into that secret place, deep within yourself, where God is present. To do this, make yourself comfortable on a chair or wherever you are most at ease. Slowly become aware of your breathing. Breathing in and breathing out, quietening down, become aware of the silent presence of God.

God breathed life into you before you were born. You are breathing twenty-four hours a day, even when you are asleep. When you stop breathing you are dead. Become conscious of your breath, and as you breathe in, become aware of the gift of life that God has given you and thank him for it. As you breathe out, surrender everything to God that blocks you being present to him: worries, sins, guilt, regrets. Let them go. Do this slowly 8–10 times.

Slowly let the words from the following psalms or any other prayer you might like fill your mind.

As a deer longs for flowing streams,
   so my soul longs for you, O God.
My soul thirsts for God,
   for the living God.
When shall I come and behold
   the face of God? (Psalm 42:1–2)

O send out your light and your truth;
   let them lead me;
let them bring me to your holy hill
   and to your dwelling.

Then I will go to the altar of God,
   to God my exceeding joy,
and I will praise you with the harp,
   O God, my God. (Psalm 43:3–4)

Alternatively, you might want to use a prayer in the spirit of Ignatius

O Christ Jesus, when all is darkness and we feel our weakness
and helplessness, give us the sense of your presence, your love and
   your strength.

Help us to have perfect trust in your protecting love and
strengthening power, so that nothing may frighten or worry us.

For, living close to you, we shall see your hand, your purpose,
   your will
through all things.
Amen.

(Prayer for trust in Jesus)

Reflection 1:

St Ignatius and
the Spiritual Exercises

Great saints were often great sinners before their conversion. Their witness or testimony can encourage us: the fact that we have made a mess of things does not mean that we have no future.

Who Was Ignatius?
Ignatius was born and grew up in Loyola in Spain. He belonged to a noble family who lived in a castle and were well off. He had a privileged upbringing.

When he grew up he wanted to be a soldier, in order to become a hero. At the age of twenty-two, he began serious military training. He had grand ideas about becoming famous, because he had also a very big ego. He enjoyed life and was sexually promiscuous. He had a violent temper and was not above the odd street brawl when challenged. No doubt, he was fond of Spanish wine and maybe something stronger. He was addicted to gambling. He had great dreams for his future.

During a battle, he was badly injured by a cannon ball. It shattered one of his legs and his knee. He had to take months out from his employment to recuperate. This was a very difficult time for him because apart from being in extreme pain, all his dreams were shattered.

During this long and painful recuperation, he got bored and looked for books to read to entertain him. Remember, there was no television or internet back then. He loved to read books of adventure and battle, and also romantic stories that kept his imagination running. None of these were available, so he had to settle for a book on the lives of the Saints and a book on the life of Jesus.

He threw his eyes up in exasperation when these were presented to him, and he left them on his bedside locker for days. Eventually he accepted that maybe reading them might be better than lying on his bed brooding. So, he started to read the lives of the saints.

These stories filled him with great joy, as had his former books on romance and chivalry. He found that under the surface these religious people were quite like him. They too wanted to do great things but in a radically different way. Gradually, he noticed something: his joy after reading the books on romance did not last for long, whereas the book on the lives of the saints gave him a lasting joy, a joy he had never experienced before.

There are two points here: one is that the type of joy he experienced from reading the lives of the saints was much deeper and lasted a long time. The second point is equally important: he *noticed* the difference in himself. *He became aware.* This only happened because he *reflected* on his experience. Because he was stuck in bed he took time to notice what went on in himself.

Ignatius realised that noticing what went on in himself like this was really important. Later he would learn that this is one of the main ways that God speaks to us. But until this point he had not been *listening* to God.

Through this process of noticing his own feelings and reactions, he slowly came to a different dream. Step by step, he began to experience how much God loved him. Now he began to dream of becoming a soldier for Christ and dedicating his life to serving God.

This was a very different journey to the one he had been on up to that point. Later he wrote about his journey so that others could discover the journey for themselves. He called his book the *Spiritual Exercises.*

We will be using some of the ideas from the *Spiritual Exercises* during this journey. Here are a few to keep in mind as we start:

- Why were we born?
- What is our purpose in life?
- What are we made for?

Ignatius gave a very short answer to these questions at the very beginning of his book. It's called 'The Principle and Foundation', by which he means 'my purpose in life'.

We are created to praise, reverence and serve God our Lord, and by this means to save our soul.

All other things on the face of the earth are created for us to help us to reach this goal.

We are to use all other things in as much as they help us to achieve this goal, and we are to refrain from using them in so far as they block us reaching our goal.

Therefore, with respect to all created things in which we have a free choice, it is necessary to become free and detached.

Our one desire should be to choose whatever helps us to reach the goal for which we are created.

So, Ignatius tells us that our main purpose in life is to live with God forever. One thing we are all sure of is that one day we will die, and as Christians we believe in a life after this one. We want to spend eternity with God. In order to do this, we need to live with God in this life. He tells us that we need to be *detached* from all things. By this he means that we have to keep our goal in mind. If we are really focused on this we will be *free* to use all things to help us get to our goal. For example, we should not fix our desires simply on achieving wealth or escaping poverty, winning success or avoiding failure, etc. Our only desire and our one choice should be what best leads us to God deepening his life in us. When we get this priority right, other things fall into place.

Ignatius tells us that we should therefore use everything at our disposal to attain that end. He calls this real freedom. Think of a youngster who wants to become a professional footballer or boxer. If he wants to get there he is going to need talent, fierce commitment and really hard work. He will have to give up lots of things to get there. He will have to train really hard, give up late nights, drugs and drinking. (How many people do you know who had a talent for sports but never made it because they went on drugs?)

In the same way, Ignatius asks us,
- What is our ultimate goal in life?
- What do we really want to do with our life?
- How do we really want to live?
- Do we really want to be free? Really free?

Keep in mind the following questions.
- Do I use everything at my disposal to achieve this goal of serving God?
- Is there anything in my life that I am very attached to, which blocks me from reaching this goal?

Do you see any connection with these questions and the first three steps of the Twelve-Step Programme?
1. We admitted we were powerless over [name your addiction], that our lives had become unmanageable.
2. We came to believe that a Power greater than ourselves could restore us to sanity.
3. We made a decision to turn our will and our lives over to the care of God *as we understand him.*

The Daily Examen or Review: Finding God in All Things
In the Spiritual Exercises Ignatius stresses that every evening we should make a review of our day. We are not looking to make a list of where we failed, nor are we checking on all our good intentions. Instead, this review is about trying to *notice* the way God has been present in our lives. (Remember how Ignatius began to see how God

was with him when he started noticing the feelings and experiences within himself.)

Start by looking back over your day and thanking God for what you were most grateful for. Remember people or events that brought you peace or joy.

Ignatius is very strong on gratitude. Gratitude is an attitude that keeps us aware of how we are blessed and of who blesses us. The Jesuit writer Tony De Mello used to say you cannot be grateful and unhappy.

There is so much to be grateful for, and we need to remind ourselves of this daily. The salvation of God is pure gift and does not depend on the merits of anyone. Everything in our life is a gift from God. How often do we thank him for what we have been given? Maybe we only think of the big things to say thanks for, but we can thank him for everything.

As we become more aware of life around us, and of creation, we will find ourselves saying thanks throughout the day. In Celtic times in Ireland, people used the prayer, 'Thanks be to God' for everything. Our gratitude is the source of our joy.

As we look back on our day, we will also notice things that were not so good. Ask God to help you deal with these. For example, maybe you met someone today and reacted badly to him or her. Noting these moments is just as important for our growth.

Allow yourself to feel your need for God. Tell God you are sorry for what you did wrong and ask for forgiveness. Each situation in your daily life provides the raw material for your prayer. Your looking back on the day becomes a way not only of meeting God, but of noticing the way God has been present with you all day, even though you may never have thought about God.

Finally, ask God to be with you tomorrow. Then you will try, with his help, to be more aware of his presence.

If you keep doing this daily review you will gradually find that you become more aware of the way God is with you all the time, and that in fact God is the greatest friend that you will ever have.

Spending Time in Prayer Each Day

A third point that Ignatius emphasises is that we should, like Jesus, spend time each day in prayer. Many people think that prayer is asking God for things all the time, or else saying prayers that we have learned, without really being aware of what we are saying. In fact, both these sorts of prayer can help. But Ignatius stresses other ways to pray that help us to become more *aware* of the way God is present to us. This will involve listening as well as talking.

Prayer is an awareness of our inner selves. It's an activity of the whole person, not just in our heads, as God is in the wholeness. Prayer involves coming to terms with silence, which turns out to be the highest form of communication. It allows you to listen more deeply to God and allows his message to penetrate your heart.

When the disciples asked Jesus to teach them how to pray, he said, 'whenever you pray, go into your room and shut the door and pray to your Father who is in secret, and your Father who sees in secret will reward you' (Matthew 6:6).

That room is deep inside each one of us. It is where God is to be found and where God speaks to us.

Then Jesus taught them the Our Father. It is good for all of us to pray this each day.

Closing Prayer: The Our Father

Reminder
- Ask yourself, 'What's my purpose in life?'
- Take the time to do a daily review.
- Make time for prayer each day.

Your Image of God

Before starting it would be helpful to read Psalm 139

Your Image of God
How would you describe the God you know?
- Is he angry, distant, caring, someone who brings you luck, stern?
- Is he someone you can relate to and who understands you?
- Does he love you?

How did you develop your image of God?
- How did you imagine God when you were a child?
- Did this image change as you got older?
- What is your image of God now?
- Is the way that you see God tied into the way you see your biological father?

How much does God matter to you?
- Is he someone very much in the background, to whom you turn in times of need, but who you then forget?
- Is God someone very important to you?
- Is God someone you would like to be important to you?
- Do you think God loves you as you are?

Who Was Jesus Christ? A Short Overview
Jesus was born as a human being over 2000 years ago. He was given his name by his parents. He went through all the pains of growing up just like you and me. His mother was Mary and his father was Joseph.

Joseph was a carpenter, and while Jesus was growing up he learned this trade from Joseph. Growing up at home he also spent a lot of time learning his prayers and the Torah (the first five books of the Old Testament Bible) and attending services in the synagogue.

All the time he was becoming more aware of God his Father in heaven, and he came to realise that he was God's Son in a very special way. After a lot of searching he felt called by his Father to leave home and go into the world with a mission to preach the Good News.

Although obviously very different, there are ways in which the world that Jesus grew up in was similar to our own today. There was a lot of corruption, injustice and inequality. Leaders cared more about business as usual than caring for the people. There were wars and conflicts. Women were treated as second-class citizens. A few people were very rich. The majority were very poor. There were self-righteous people who looked down on 'sinners' and considered themselves above everyone else.

The message that Jesus shared was good news because he declared that God created this world for *everyone*. He taught that we were all God's children, equal in his eyes. We all had an equal right to the produce of the earth. We all had an equivalent dignity. It didn't matter what our religious background, gender or class, nationality or race was. He challenged the tax collectors, the religious leaders, the cultural elites and the Romans who were occupying Israel – everyone who used their strength to take advantage of the poor. He radically sided with people who were marginalised and scorned.

He showed great compassion and forgiveness to the 'sinners' of society. He healed the sick. On reflection, those around him realised he was love itself.

Those in power both in 'Church' and 'state' were very threatened by his message and tried various ways to catch him out. He always came back with a deeper question that flummoxed them. When they didn't succeed, they decided to kill him. They plotted a false case against him. They were successful and this ended up with Jesus being arrested, prosecuted and sentenced to death on a cross. The last night of his life was spent in prison, stitched up by people who could not or would not comprehend his message.

Read about Jesus' passion and death (Matthew 27). He was innocent, but nonetheless he was accused and brought before a court. There was a judge. False witnesses accused him of blasphemy.

Jesus understands the suffering of those in prison because he has experienced it. Jesus understands the suffering of those in the real 'prison' of addiction. Jesus shares in our suffering.

Too often we pass over this remarkable claim that Christianity makes: God was a prisoner. Despite being utterly innocent, he was found guilty and sentenced to be crucified to death on a cross.

This was the worst kind of sentence you could receive. Abandoned by many of his friends, he was left in the hands of a brutal criminal justice system without representation. Before they crucified him, they scourged and beat him until he bled. They stripped him naked and humiliated him. Then they put the cross on his shoulder and made him walk through the streets to Calvary while the people jeered at him.

When you die on a cross, you actually suffocate under your own body weight. It is a slow and excruciating death. It is torture. Can you imagine what that must have been like? Before he carried his cross he was so badly beaten that he was weak and already near death.

There were three crosses on Calvary. Jesus hung in the middle. On each side of him was a prisoner who had also been sentenced to death on a cross. They were guilty of theft, among other crimes. One of the prisoners repented. When he looked at Jesus, he recognised that he was the Son of God and he asked him to remember him when he came into his kingdom. Jesus forgave him there and then and told him that he would be with him in paradise that very day.

Jesus suffered and died so that each of us might be saved, live life to the full and go to heaven when we die.

The story of Jesus is the story of how much God loves each of us. It is a love story. Each of us is worth so much to God that he himself became human in order to suffer with us in a real way, in flesh and blood. The powerful forces of injustice in society could not handle this man. He was an enigma: a leader who went into battle for the sake of the weak and forgotten, with no weapons beyond the truth and his own goodness; a preacher who understood just how bad humans could be and insisted nevertheless that God's mercy was wider; a philosopher who unravelled the mysteries of existence in short stories and gave us the wisdom to live well. He was all these things and more. He was fully God and fully human.

What God becomes, God redeems. Because of Jesus, we don't have to pretend we are better than we are. We can confess ours sins and know that we will not be rejected. Because of Jesus we need never again despair. The cross reminds us that even the worst thing in the world is not the end of the story.

Crucifixion, it turns out, was not the end of Jesus. The suffering that he endured and his savage death were not meaningless. They turned out to be the most meaningful thing that had ever happened. All the force and brutality and corrupt power humanity had at its disposal was spent killing this prince of peace. All the injustice of the world was poured out on his body and at first it appeared as if it had crushed him. He died. His friends despaired (though some women stayed courageously faithful to the end).

Three days later, he came back from the dead. He was not resuscitated, which would imply he would die again. He was *resurrected*. His amazed friends, the terrified Romans and soon the whole world were to discover that death was just the beginning. He lived. He lives still. He spent six more weeks with his friends teaching them how the good news affects life here and now. Then he returned to his Father in heaven, leaving us his Spirit, through whom we can have access to God to this day.

How It All Started
Read John 1:35–39, where we learn about Jesus' first meeting with his followers, Andrew and an unnamed disciple. At the end of this reading take time to reflect. Can you take time to hear Jesus asking you, 'What do you want?'

> The next day John again was standing with two of his disciples, and as he watched Jesus walk by he exclaimed, 'Look,

here is the Lamb of God!' The two disciples heard him say this, and they followed Jesus. When Jesus turned and saw them following, he said to them, 'What do you want?' They said to him, 'Rabbi' (which translated means Teacher), 'where are you staying?' He said to them, 'Come and see'. They came and saw where he was staying, and they remained with him that day. (Matthew 1:35–39)

Jesus asked the two men, 'What do you want?' Can you take time to hear Jesus ask you the same question? Do not rush your answer. Your first answer may be very superficial. For some in prison the first answer is often, 'I want to get out of here'. When they get out, however, they celebrate by drinking alcohol and taking other drugs and are back inside before they know it. For people outside of prison, the first answer is often, 'I need to stop drinking alcohol or taking other drugs'. Yet, they take some the next day.

An alcoholic once said to me, 'If I had another drink I would be able to think straight!' So, you may have to go deeper to find the answer.

Maybe you need to hear God ask you, 'What do you want?' Even then you may have to go deeper still to get the true and sometimes difficult answer.

What Do You Really, Really, Really Want?

There are two great Christian truths about desire. The first is that God desires us. So we pray to have a deep appreciation that God desires us and wants to share his life and his love with each of us. God has an intense desire to help us achieve the end for which we were lovingly created. God has a real desire for my life, for what becomes of me.

The second is that we are invited to desire what God desires, and in doing so we find the long-term shape of our lives. *What do you want?*

Consider prayer. You can pray for insight into what God desires for you. You can pray to experience and treasure the depths of your desire for God. Even recognising this desire is itself a deep form of prayer.

29

Look at the following steps of the Twelve-Step Programme:

4. Made a searching and fearless moral inventory of ourselves.
5. Admitted to God, to ourselves and to another human being the exact nature of our wrongs.
6. Were entirely ready to have God remove all these defects of character.
7. Humbly ask God to remove our shortcomings.
8. Made a list of all persons we had harmed and became willing to make amends to them all.
9. Made direct amends to such people wherever possible, except when to do so would injure them or others.
10. Continued to take personal inventory and when we were wrong, promptly admitted it.
11. Sought through prayer and meditation to improve our conscious contact with God as we understood him, praying only for knowledge of his will for us and the power to carry that out.

Closing Prayer: The Our Father

Reminder
- Ask yourself, 'What's my purpose in life?'
- Make time for daily prayer and review.
- Hear God ask you, 'What do you want?'

The Negative Forces of Sin in the World

The Prodigal Son

The story of the prodigal son first tells us about a son who went off the rails. In our next reflection we will see how his father responds.

This is an important story and one that you should spend much time on. Christians often spend their whole lives studying and pondering this profound tale. It is one of those stories that you can keep turning over and over to see new perspectives.

In the Spiritual Exercises, Ignatius recommends that you first read a passage of scripture and then imagine that you are present in the scene it describes. You might see yourself looking on as Jesus performs a miracle or preaches. You might even imagine yourself as one of the characters in the story, like the prodigal son or his father.

Notice how you feel. What questions come up for you? See if your life connects with the story in any way.

This is first part of the story of the prodigal son:

> There was a man who had two sons. The younger of them said to his father, 'Father, give me the share of the wealth that will belong to me.' So he divided his assets between them. A few days later the younger son gathered all he had and travelled to a distant region, and there he squandered his wealth in wild living. When he had spent everything, a severe famine took place throughout that region, and he began to be in need. So he went and hired himself out to one of the citizens of that region, who sent him to his fields to feed the pigs. He would gladly have filled his stomach with the pods that the pigs were

eating, and no one gave him anything. But when he came to his senses he said, 'How many of my father's hired hands have bread enough and to spare, but here I am dying of hunger! I will get up and go to my father, and I will say to him, 'Father, I have sinned against heaven and before you; I am no longer worthy to be called your son; treat me like one of your hired hands.'

So he set off and went to his father. (Luke 15:11–20)

Freedom NOW!

The prodigal son was unhappy. He wanted FREEDOM. So he looked for his inheritance so that he could go off and enjoy life. He wanted everything NOW. He couldn't wait till his father died. So the father gave him his inheritance, because God the Father gives us our freedom.

How often do you want things and want them NOW?

He got his money and went off to a distant land. There he started partying, drinking, taking drugs, gambling, having sex, drifting from one job to the next, getting fired, telling lies, covering up, cheating, etc. He had a great time. This is how he understood freedom.

Did you live it up in order to be cool and be one of the gang? What do you think you were really looking for? Could it be a sense of direction, a purpose or meaning in life? Was it happiness and fulfilment or something else that you were looking for?

There are some questions that Google won't answer, and you have to turn somewhere deep inside yourself for the answers.

The story tells us that in choosing to spend all his money on wine, women and song, the prodigal son lost everything. 'Prodigal' means wasteful, after all. I wonder what that was like for him? He

- lost his money, his job and any prospect of getting one;
- lost his friends and family;
- lost his self-respect and self-belief.
- He hit rock bottom: he ended up in a pigsty eating with the pigs.

Does this sound familiar? Many people who are addicted tell a similar story.

What pigsty have you ended up in because of your addiction? Are you in prison or going back to prison? Maybe you aren't in prison, but you are imprisoned by your addiction.

The consequences of addiction can include:

- physical, emotional and sexual abuse,
- domestic violence,
- loss of job, increased debts,
- loss of marriage and children, loss of relationships, family,
- more violence, more crime,
- road accidents due to reckless driving,
- toxicity of the body and damage to the organs including liver, brain and central nervous system,
- increased risk of homelessness,
- suicide.

Is that what you really, really want?

Associations with Addiction

In the story we are told that the son came to his senses. I wonder what that was like? Did he get a wake-up call? Did he start thinking and asking some questions? Did he ask himself 'What direction is my life taking? Will my present behaviour get me to where I want to go?'

Some questions you might want to ask yourself:

- Do you ever think of the consequences of your alcohol drinking and other drug taking?
- Do you see it as a sin?
- Do you think of all the children in school today, maybe some of your own, who will go home to a parent drunk or addicted to other drugs lying on the couch in a catatonic state?
- Do you think of the children who will go without food tonight because the money has been spent on alcohol and/or other drugs?

- Do you think of the women and men who will be beaten up tonight or raped because of alcohol and other drug abuse?
- Do you think of the next on the list to get murdered because the drug addict can't pay the dealer for their drugs?
- Do you think of the next car accident by a drunken driver who is going to leave someone dead and a family shattered?
- Do you think of all the people whose lives have been irrevocably damaged because of the abuse of alcohol and other drugs through everyday muggings, robberies and other crimes, often on the most vulnerable in our society like the elderly?
- Do you think of all who have ended up in prison because of what alcohol and other drugs did to them before they had the wit to walk away?
- Do you think of the harm suffered by those close to you – parents, spouses or partners, children, friends and many more – because of your addiction?

Probably not. Because usually those addicted to alcohol and other drugs are thinking more about themselves and the next drink or drug, than anyone else. A core trait of those in addiction is selfishness. When you think of alcohol and other drugs, instead of thinking about the consequences, are you more likely to think something like the following?

My addictions:

- Help ME to relax.
- Help ME to feel good.
- Help ME to feel I can deal with things better in my life.
- Help ME deal with my depression and anxiety better.
- Help ME to have a good time and enjoy the craic.
- Help ME to get away from people who drive me crazy.
- Help ME get rid of all my worries, pain, anger, resentment, the whole works, all gone when I get high.

How much of ME is involved in all this?

Addictive substances may do all or some of that at first. But, as you know, the more you take, the greater the tolerance you build. Then you need more and more to reach the same relaxed feeling. By this time, you are hooked.

Do you remember the first time that you really got absolutely high? Do you remember the marvellous feeling? But has that ever happened since?

The drugs change our brains. That's why we feel good.

Is that cool? Remember, a lot of people started to drink and take drugs because it was cool.

Our association of addiction with pleasure needs to be broken and replaced with reality. The reality of addiction is losing:

- my job,
- my marriage,
- my children,
- my health,
- my self-respect,
- my integrity, and, for some,
- ending up in prison for things they never wanted to do in the first place.

Changing the association of addiction from pleasure to reality leads to the beginning of inner freedom. The urge to take drugs weakens. We may begin to seek help, but changing the association is never easy.

We are surrounded by a culture, strongly influenced by advertising, that wants us to think of pleasure when we think of alcohol and other drugs, and even wealth and power. Ads may carry a health warning in small print, but they will never spell out the long-term side effects that addiction can cause. Alcohol, drugs, power and wealth are depicted as positive things in our society. We talk about how drinking alcohol is embedded in our 'cultural DNA'.

Deep Down, What Do You Really Want?

Despite greater prosperity in Ireland, there are a lot of very unhappy and lonely people. A lot of this is due to the fact that people have sought meaning and fulfilment in the wrong areas. Many in addiction, when they come down from their high and find all their problems are still there, talk about a restlessness in their lives, an emptiness within and a constant need to fill that emptiness, always looking for something more. This longing, which is a fundamental, unconscious driving force, has great power.

People with addictions often try to fill their emptiness with alcohol or other drugs. As they slowly discover that this won't work, they increase their intake in the hope that it will, only to discover that it never does. By then, they have developed a craving for the substance and a dependency on it. This in turn cuts them off further from that spiritual drive that allows them to reflect and function in a unified way. They become enslaved to their compulsion.

Addiction is a unique experience for everyone. Each person's story is different. But many, when they start on the road to recovery, often experience a duality in themselves. They feel like they have two parts or two selves pulling at each other.

One part is the child, adolescent or old self, who started using alcohol and other drugs as a way to find pleasure or as a flight from pain, abuse and stress. In the process that self discovers that these addictive substances don't agree with him or her and lead him or her into very destructive behaviours.

The other part is the new, wiser self, who has used their rational mind and realised that addiction is messing up their life, and that they had better stop and start to make some self-caring decisions.

The conflict between these two selves often gets worse, leading to inner turmoil, broken promises, guilt, harmful consequences and a reduced capacity to be satisfied from the ordinary pleasures of life.

The association of addiction with pleasure is still alive and well and very tempting. It's often all we know. Up to now it has killed the pain, albeit for a short time. However, we have to give up what once felt like the solution and retrain our brains to believe survival comes with new behaviour.

Most people will require help to overcome their addiction. AA is one option but counselling and/or residential treatment are others. So, *what do you really want?*

The change you are looking for is not going to come from outside yourself, but rather from within. You have to go to the core of your being.

You have to go on what I call a soul journey, to discover who and what you are beneath the addiction and distorted behaviour patterns you may have developed.

This means reasserting your trust in yourself, in others and in God. It is about finding out: Who am I? What does the gift of life mean to me? Where do I now want to go with my life? What is my purpose in life? This will involve:

- First admitting you have a problem with alcohol and other drugs or gambling or whatever your addiction may be,
- Acknowledging that you are sick and need help,
- Admitting the truth – no more lies, no more fooling yourself or thinking you are fooling others. The truth will be your first step towards freedom. Many in addiction mask who they are and what they really want or think, because they fear rejection. Yet pretence of any kind – either to yourself or to others – denies you your full potential.

Most of us never take the time or patience to do this. Instead we have learned not to listen to our spiritual voice and to just act in the moment on impulse, without stopping to think of the consequences of our actions. These external influences create a lot of noise, which blocks out the whispers from our soul that tell us what we really need and what we really value. Living from the soul is living true to who we are and to our own values.

Go back again to the 'Principle and Foundation' or 'my purpose in life' in Reflection 1. It may not have made much sense to you when you read it first, but do you now see a connection between it and your life?

What attachment is blocking your freedom? Consider AA's Daily Examination:

1. If we are faced with a situation that provides us with the option of being either selfish or unselfish, which option do we choose?
2. Do we allow ourselves to be concerned about the needs and welfare of someone else or do we instinctively put our own needs first?
3. Do we ever wonder whether our spouse or other family members are happy or sad, sick or well, or are we still preoccupied with ourselves?
4. Are we taking the risk of expressing and presenting ourselves honestly or are we still trying to be people pleasers in order to gain approval from other people – even at the expense of our own dignity and self-respect?
5. Are we being tolerant of the shortcomings and mistakes of others or are we being judgmental and spending more time taking the inventory of others rather than our own?
6. Are we exercising patience in our daily affairs or are we still childishly hanging on to the 'want what I want when I want it' approach to life?
7. Are we beginning to accept the responsibility for our own behaviour and are we promptly admitting when we are wrong or are we continuing to alibi, justify or blame others for our mistakes?
8. Have we let go of our old resentments or are we still nursing them along, allowing them to feed on self-pity? Have we come to realize that harbouring resentment hurts us more than anyone else and self-pity is only a step away from drinking alcohol or using other drugs?
9. Are we dealing with current problems today or do we find ourselves still tending to manipulate or procrastinate without considering how our lack of action can affect others?
10. Are we looking at ourselves and life situations realistically or are we still expecting more of ourselves and of life than we have a

right to, thus risking disappointment, frustration, and a return to alcohol or other drugs?

11. 'Thy will be done not mine'.

Closing Prayer: The Our Father

Reminder

- Keep asking 'What's my purpose in life?' and keep practising the daily review and daily prayer.
- Listen for God asking you, 'What do you want?'
- A simple, powerful prayer to consider, 'Lord be merciful to me, a sinner'.

Reflection 4:

Despite My Sinfulness,
I Am Loved by God

What Is God's Wish for Us?

God's wish is for us to be happy, joyous and free. What does that mean?

Ignatius began to look at his inner world of thoughts, feelings, moods and desires. He noticed inner spiritual movements. His spiritual feelings had lasting, positive effects on him. The good feelings that came from thinking of his own glory and success, these didn't last.

Does addiction give us lasting happiness?

We saw in the last exercise that the prodigal son decided to make that long journey home and return to his father. In the next part of the story we see how the father received him. You might expect his father to beat him up or throw him out, but read the story to see what really happened:

The Father of the Prodigal Son

> So he set off and went to his father. But while he was still far off, his father saw him and was filled with compassion; he ran and put his arms around him and kissed him. Then the son said to him, 'Father, I have sinned against heaven and before you; I am no longer worthy to be called your son.' But the father said to his slaves, 'Quickly, bring out a robe – the best one – and put it on him; put a ring on his finger and sandals on his feet. And get the fatted calf and kill it, and let us eat and celebrate, for this son of mine was dead and is alive again; he was lost and is found!' And they began to celebrate. (Luke 15:20–24)

Questions

It was Jesus who told the story. He wanted to give his people some idea of what his Father was like. His Father was his God. Jesus called him his 'Abba'. In English that would be something like 'Daddy'.

- How do you think God, your Father, would receive you if you decided to return to him?
- What would returning to him involve?
- Do you think that he would greet you with open arms?
- What would it be like if he did?
- Do you think you could trust him? Remember how Jesus' tale suggests he is full of love and mercy!
- How do you think the image of God in your head is different from the way that God is in reality? (Go back again to Reflection 2, where it was noted that your image of God may be confused by your image of your own father).
- What would it mean for the way you live your life if God was different and better than you had ever imagined?

Recovery and the Journey Home

Do you have a choice? You always have a choice. You can choose to continue to follow your addiction despite the cost to you and those around you, or you can choose to turn around and make that journey back to freedom. You have to make your own choice and take responsibility for it. No more blaming others or making excuses.

- It will be your choice whether to go to AA, or counselling or a treatment programme.
- It will be your choice whether or not you decide to turn your life back to prayer, which many in addiction have found helpful in the past.
- It will be your choice to hold on to the resentment, jealousy, anger and hurt, or whatever you blame for your addiction.
- It will be your choice to do nothing about your life and instead continue the self-abuse.

Read the following poem, 'Autobiography in Five Short Chapters'.

Chapter 1
I walk down the street.
There is a deep hole in the side walk.
I fall in.
I am lost … I am helpless.
It isn't my fault.
It takes forever to find a way out.

Chapter 2
I walk down the same street.
There is a deep hole in the side walk.
I *pretend* I don't see it.
I fall in again.
I can't believe I am in the same place,
but, it isn't my fault.
It still takes a long time to get out.

Chapter 3
I walk down the same street.
There is a deep hole in the side walk.
I see it is there.
I still fall in … **It's a habit.**
My eyes are open.
I know where I am.
It is my fault.
I get out immediately.

Chapter 4
I walk down the same street.
There is a deep hole in the side walk.
I walk around it.

Chapter 5
I walk down another street.

From *There's a Hole in My Sidewalk*: *The Romance of Self-Discovery* by Portia Nelson.

From the time we are born until we die, we go through different stages of development, from babyhood, to childhood, to teenager years, to early adulthood, adulthood, mid-life and old age.

At each stage or chapter in our development we learn more about life and especially about ourselves. We become aware of our strengths and weaknesses. We reflect on the choices we have made and think about the choices we can make for the future. We realise that there are behavioural changes we may need to make, as we enter the next stage or chapter of our lives.

In the early stages of our development we are exploring, testing and finding out what we can and cannot do.

As children we learn that if we put our fingers into the fire, we will get burned. So we stop thinking of doing it.

As teenagers we know we are moving out of childhood and into adulthood. We can go through a phase where we think we know everything and no longer need direction or guidance. We are still experimenting. Hopefully we learn from our experiences as to what we should and should not do. This is often the stage when we start to experiment with alcohol and other drugs and initially see no harm in either.

As we move into early adulthood we begin to make further changes. We may now be in the workplace. We are interested in romantic relationships, leaving our home and family of origin and perhaps even forming our own families. This requires moving into a more respon-sible stage or chapter in our development. We become responsible human beings and become responsible for the other people we may bring into the world. This will require leaving the carefree behaviour of the teenage years behind and taking on new levels of responsible behaviour. The rewards of doing this well are immense but hard to understand in advance.

Then, as we mature in life, we will be faced with new challenges and new behaviours that will require us to behave in all sorts of new and challenging ways.

Unfortunately, during these stages of development, some of us can get stuck at a certain stage or chapter and do not move on to the next stage. We can find people in their adult lives acting and behaving like teenagers: refusing to take on the responsibilities and behaviours of mature adults and instead continuing to act out in very immature ways.

Some important questions to ask yourself are:

- Have you become stuck along the way?
- Do you keep falling into the same hole?
- Do you keep pretending you don't see it, or keep telling yourself it isn't your fault? If so might you still be stuck at Chapter Two, still acting like a teenager?
- Has your addiction become a habit that has crept up on you, but you are now beginning to see the consequences?
- What different street do you need to walk down from here on? What changes would that require from you?
- Where are you in the journey outlined in that story?

Jesus' Prayer in the Light of the Story of the Prodigal Father

The story, as we have seen, is about a self-centred son who left his father and got completely lost.

When he came to his senses, he thought he was an outcast. His father (representing God) surprised him with the truth that he could never be separated from God's love.

When he returned home he was welcomed way beyond his wildest hopes. His father ran up to him, threw his arms around him and kissed him, while the best the son had hoped for was to become his father's servant.

This is the kind of Daddy you pray to when you say 'Our Father'. He is better than anyone you ever met in this world. When you pray the Our Father, see yourself as the prodigal son returning home..

See the Father standing there with open arms and gifts way beyond what any drink or drug could give you. This is the Father we turn to in prayer. As you talk to him become aware that there is nothing you need to hide, nothing you cannot share, be it anger, resentment, guilt or fear.

Give thanks that you have a lover like God. Thank him that he cared so much for you that he waited for you and sent his beloved Son into the world to die on the cross for you, to rise again and rescue you from your demons; and all this long before you thought of turning to him.

Ask that you may know what he wants of you, and that you will be able to do it.

Ask him for what you really need, and not for everything that you want.

Remember all your own sins and failures. Ask the Lord for forgiveness for all of these. Ask him to forgive you just as the prodigal father forgave his son. There is no limit to God's forgiveness.

Pray also that you may be able to forgive, that you may move towards freedom by letting go of all the anger towards others for the suffering they have caused you. Letting go of past hurts is really hard. Most people need help to do it. Ask the Lord to help you. Then you can be free of your guilt, anguish and pain.

We address God as 'our' and not 'my' because he is Daddy to all of us, and we are all his children, all equal, unique and loved in his sight. Therefore, we must see each other as brothers and sisters and love each other.

Ask that he may guide and direct you, that he will lead you into the right road. In the 'Hole in the Road' story, remember the final chapter – real freedom is achieved by finding a new street to walk down, away from potential harm.

We are not alone in that task. When we ask God to steer us away from temptation, what we are really seeking is that he would steer us into safe and healthy paths.

Ask him to protect you from all the forces of evil in the world.

In our modern age, people often laugh at the idea of evil. But many of us, if we are honest, know that we have brushed up against demons within ourselves that are stronger than us.

Ask to be protected from anxiety, depression and for freedom from addiction.

We need God's help. We can become monsters without God, and so we ask for the protection that God wishes to give us.

Open yourself to the reality of your Father so that the love, power, strength and protection of God begin to enter your life and transform you.

At the end of each reflection pray the Our Father. This is Jesus' own prayer, the prayer Jesus taught his disciples when they asked him to teach them to pray.

Keep that image of the prodigal father in your mind as you say the prayer.

The Prodigal Girl

Some people think that it is only men who suffer from addiction. In fact, a huge number of women also suffer. They may find the following poem helpful. It talks about 'the prodigal girl' instead of the 'prodigal boy'.

Great poets have sung the beauties of home,
Its comforts, its love and its joy;
How back to the place of its sheltering dome
We welcome the prodigal boy.

They picture his father with pardoning smile
And glittering robes to unfurl;
But none of the poets thought it worthwhile
To sing of the prodigal girl.

The prodigal son can resume his old place
As leader of fashion's mad whirl,

With never a hint of his former disgrace
Not so for the prodigal girl.

The girl may come back to the home she had left
But nothing is ever the same;
The shadow still lingers o'er the dear ones bereft
Society scoffs at her name.

Perhaps that is why the prodigal girl
Gets lost on life's devious tract;
She thinks of the lips that will scornfully curl
And hasn't the heart to turn back.

Yes, welcome the prodigal son to his place;
Kill the calf, fill the free-flowing bowl;
But shut not the door on his frail sister's face,
Remember, she too has a soul.

'The Prodigal Girl', Anonymous

Closing Prayer: The Our Father

Reminder
- Keep asking 'What's my purpose in life?' and keep practising the daily Examen and daily prayer.
- Listen for God asking you, 'What do you want?'
- Remember that you are a loved sinner, 'Lord be merciful to me, a sinner'.
- Do you need to walk down a different street?

Reflection 5:

God's Mercy and Healing

Healing Your Pain
Your pain: what's it like?
- What pain have you got in your life?
- Do you suffer from anxiety, depression or other mental health issues?
- Are you lonely?
- Are you angry or resentful?
- Have you been given a bad deal?
- Do you hate being in prison or allowing alcohol or other drugs create your own prison outside?
- Are you afraid? If so, of what?

Remember, these questions are for yourself. Others will not know your answers unless you tell them. But could you tell Jesus what your answers are? Jesus was great at healing people during his ministry. Can you ask him to heal you? Can you become aware of all this pain?

The following is a story of one of the many healings that Jesus carried out in his life. Could he do the same for you?

The Story of the Paralytic
One day while he was teaching, Pharisees and teachers of the law who had come from every village of Galilee and Judea and from Jerusalem were sitting nearby, and the power of the Lord was with him to heal. Just then some men came carrying a paralyzed man on a stretcher. They were trying to bring him in and lay him before Jesus, but, finding no way to bring him in because of the crowd, they went up on the

roof and let him down on the stretcher through the tiles into the middle of the crowd in front of Jesus. When he saw their faith, he said, 'Friend, your sins are forgiven you.' Then the scribes and the Pharisees began to question, 'Who is this who is speaking blasphemies? Who can forgive sins but God alone?' When Jesus perceived their questionings, he answered them, 'Why do you raise such questions in your hearts? Which is easier: to say, "Your sins are forgiven you", or to say, "Stand up and walk"? But so that you may know that the Son of Man has authority on earth to forgive sins' – he said to the one who was paralyzed – 'I say to you, stand up and take your stretcher and go to your home.' Immediately he stood up before them, took what he had been lying on, and went to his home, glorifying God. Amazement seized all of them, and they glorified God and were filled with fear, saying, 'We have seen incredible things today.' (Luke 5:17–26)

All of us need healing in our lives at different times, and it is important to pray for it. Most of the people suffering from addiction that I have accompanied have found spiritual healing massively important, although spiritual healing meant something different to many of them. For some it was explicitly religious, for others it involved getting in touch with a deeper aspect of a relationship or becoming more aware of beauty in nature or in music. In all cases they were touching in to a part of themselves that was deeper than reason. When things get straightened out in our soul, it is so much easier to get our mind and body together as well. Experience shows that physical and psychological healings received through deeper reflection include a spiritual healing. All of us have experienced inner sufferings or conflicts. For Christians, we know from the Bible that Jesus can heal us, not only physically but also psychologically, emotionally and spiritually.

Ask yourself:

- Who or what paralyses you in your life, in your relationships?
- Are you paralysed by fear, doubts, shame, negative thinking, selfishness, pride, a low self-image, addictions, feeling that you are worthless in God's eyes?
- What do you need healing from now in your life? Tell Jesus.
- Do you need healing from past hurts? Maybe you were rejected, abused, bullied, harmed?
- Maybe you felt you were never listened to or understood and this left you feeling inadequate or with low self-esteem?
- Maybe you need healing from depression and/or anxiety or from addiction?
- Maybe you have to heal your distorted image of God, who is not a harsh judge, or a Santa Clause, but a loving Father, Friend and Brother?
- Are you still stuck in the past and see no way out?
- Do you feel you cannot change your life?
- What would it be like to start believing that things can change? We know we cannot change the past, but we can have a different future. What could your future be?
- Could you start by asking God in your prayers to guide and direct you?

A Prayer of Ignatius of Loyola for Depression

O Christ Jesus,
when all is darkness
and we feel our weakness and helplessness,
give us the sense of Your presence,
Your love, and Your strength.
Help us to have perfect trust
in Your protecting love
and strengthening power,
so that nothing may frighten or worry us,
for, living close to You,

we shall see Your hand,
Your purpose, Your will through all things.

Revisit

Go back and read Reflections 1 and 2 again:

- What is the centre of your life when you live with addiction?
- How do you displace God?
- What gifts, talents, people, possessions have you received from God? Can you list them?
- What has proved helpful or a hindrance in your life to becoming a loving person?
- Are you open to change?
- Are you open to trusting God despite your fears and anxieties?

Prisoners of the Past

Pope Francis has spoken again and again about the need for prisoners never to lose hope or fall into the temptation that they can never be forgiven. In his homily for the Jubliee of Mercy: Jubilee for Prisoners in St Peter's Basilica on 6 November 2016, he said, 'Hope is a gift of God … Whenever someone makes a mistake, the Father's mercy is all the more present, awakening repentance, forgiveness, reconciliation, and peace.'

> If God hopes, then no one should lose hope. For hope is the strength to keep moving forward. It is the power to press on towards the future and a changed life. It is the incentive to look to tomorrow, so that the love we have known, for all our failings, can show us a new path.

People in prison should not be held 'captive' by their past mistakes, and should 'never yield to the temptation of thinking that we cannot be forgiven'.

You don't have to be in prison for alcohol and other drugs to imprison you. You may be in your own prison outside from these drugs.

Closing Prayer: The Our Father

Reminder
- Keep reflecting on 'my purpose in life' and keep practising the daily Examen and daily prayer.
- Keep listening for God's question, 'What do you want?'
- Keep in mind that you are a loved sinner.
- Do you need to walk down a different street?
- What do you need healing from?

Love of God and Love of Self

God's Love for Us

'Listen! I am standing at the door, knocking; if you hear my voice and open the door, I will come in and eat with you, and you with me' (Revelation 3:20).

Jesus has been standing, knocking at the door of our hearts with infinite patience, and he will continue to do so until the end of our lives. It is never too late to open that door and invite him into our lives.

Prayer

Lord we do not understand why you love us so much and why you are so patient with us. It can only be because you are love itself. Help us to hear that persistent knocking and to open ourselves to you.

Jesus always leaves us free to respond or not, because his relationship with us is one of love. To those who want to find him, he says, 'Come and meet me in real prayer and open your hearts to me.' Jesus, you are telling each of us to come and see, help us to truly meet you in prayer and to discover the joy of coming to know and love you.

This is how we come to know him personally, and it leads us to loving him and following him.

Ignatius, in the Spiritual Exercises, like Jesus, found that spending time in prayer every day was very important. (Remember what we said in Reflection 1).

Take a Moment to Think

For a moment imagine you are in a cell in prison or at home in your house. There is a knock at the door and you are told there is someone here to see you. His name is Jesus.

Jesus stands at the door and smiles at you. He asks if he can come in. You bring him in. Slowly you find yourself chatting with him about everything in your life. You start with your childhood, growing up in your family, school, your friends, your work, all the way to now.

As you talk with him you begin to realise that he knows everything about you, and that he was present in all your experiences and was nudging you, challenging you, helping and beckoning you along the way, but you were not aware of him.

You discover that everything in your life seems to mean something to him. You begin to discover that not only does he know everything that you have gone through, but he also walked every step of the way with you, allowing you to make your own choices.

Talking to him changes the way you see things. You begin to realise that he is right here with you and wishing you would talk to him more.

He is looking at you. Notice he is looking at you with eyes filled with love and humility. You hear him say, 'I love and accept you just as you are. You do not have to change for me to offer you my love. You don't have to become better, or to give up your sins. Obviously I would want you to do so. But that's not a condition for receiving my love and acceptance. You have that already, before you change, even if you never decide to change at all. Do you believe me? Do you believe that I accept and love you as you are, and not as you should be, or may become someday? But, of course, to let my love enter into you, you will have to change. Ponder what I'm saying to you and tell me what you really feel.'

How Does Jesus Feel about Us?
Read this passage. It is from John 15:9–17:

> As the Father has loved me, so I have loved you; abide in my love. If you keep my commandments, you will abide in my love, just as I have kept my Father's commandments and abide in his love. I have said these things to you so that my joy may be in you and that your joy may be complete.
>
> 'This is my commandment, that you love one another as I have loved you. No one has greater love than this, to lay down one's

life for one's friends. You are my friends if you do what I command you. I do not call you servants any longer, because the servant does not know what the master is doing, but I have called you friends, because I have made known to you everything that I have heard from my Father. You did not choose me, but I chose you. And I appointed you to go and bear fruit, fruit that will last, so that the Father will give you whatever you ask him in my name. I am giving you these commands so that you may love one another.

How We See Ourselves

Many people who are addicted have a very low opinion of themselves. Many feel inadequate in lots of ways, anxious, fearful, powerless or depressed. For some, these feelings can also be an underlying cause for their excessive drinking, drug taking, eating disorders, self-harm, etc.

While the alcohol and other drugs blot out these feelings for a while, they also make these feelings worse when the alcohol and other drugs wear off. People who suffer from depression often turn to alcohol to lift it. While it does so initially, they fail to recognise that alcohol is a depressant and in the long term will only make their depression worse. Likewise, other drugs leave people feeling more anxious and with panic attacks. Some end up having delusions or paranoia. Liam Gallagher, the singer, recently spoke about the panic attacks he suffered as a result of heroin use.

Low self-esteem is often not seen as an underlying issue in addiction. Yet people who use alcohol or other drugs to help their self-esteem end up with two problems: addiction and an even lower view of themselves.

Many instances of low self-esteem have their origin in our childhood experiences. It is of course true that some may have had a childhood that gave them every reason to trust in life and in themselves, and yet they fail to do so. Others feel small because they were constantly put down as children at home or in school. Some had bad experiences of parents fighting and drinking, or they were bullied, unjustly punished or abused.

Older people often speak about their childhoods, when they had things hard. Nobody listened to them. They were never asked for their opinion. They were treated as objects. Now they have grown up to believe that they are no good, that they don't have a worthwhile opinion. In today's world, many young people *appear* full of self-confidence, but when you peel away the layers you find they have many doubts about themselves and their abilities as people.

How self-confident are you – underneath all the slagging?

Self-Esteem and Faith: I Am a Child of God

A Christian is meant to see things differently. We are meant to value our dignity and uniqueness as persons made in the image of God. I have an undeniable God-given value. We are called to trust in ourselves and in God who accepts and supports us as we are. This should lead to us feeling valuable as persons in spite of all our limitations.

Before we can get this kind of spiritual awareness of our self-worth, which I believe we get through faith, prayer and trust in God, we have to face our own psychological reality in life and how our own sense of self was formed.

I have to face up to how my low self-image has affected me, how it continues to affect me and to determine the way I live my life. I need to look at my life history and at all the experiences I have had that left me believing I was no good. These experiences may block me from getting into that deeper place within myself, where I can experience being loved by God.

If I cannot love myself then I cannot imagine that God loves me. If I'm holding an image of my father who bullied me or abused me, and I see God the Father in the same way, then I will have a problem experiencing God's love.

We have to face what life has dished out to us, but we will find ultimate healing at the spiritual level where we meet a God who loves us deeply and sees us as fantastic, despite all our flaws. When we reach that place we won't worry about our self-image.

A poor self-image is a block to our appreciating our own humanity. It makes us focus on ourselves and on our sinful tendencies and disappointments. It blinds us to the goodness of God, who made us, and who mercifully continues to save us.

The scriptures tell us that our 'real' image is 'like unto God' for whom we exist. Our hope and confidence are not in ourselves as sinners, but in Christ our saviour, in whom we exist and without whom we are nothing.

In the creation story in Genesis we are told that we were made in the 'image and likeness of God' (Genesis 1:26). Whether we are trying to or not, there is something about humans that reflects God back into the world. This is never earned by any behaviour or reputation, ritual or achievement. It is something that we can come to recognise in ourselves and others, but it is never about meeting some human list of qualifications (Ephesians: 2:8–10).

We can only begin to claim our innate goodness when we grasp the love of our Creator and the truth of creation, which shows us the infinite goodness of God. Only when we focus on the goodness of God the Creator, who made us, can we acknowledge the 'wonder of our being'.

We are talking about *God's* goodness in us and not our own. God found the work of his hands very good. It is true that our sinfulness spoils our likeness to God, and we must repent for this, but nothing can destroy the goodness that God has made. Despite all our failings we are good, because God made us in God's image.

To deny our goodness is to deny God, the source of all goodness. To deny the goodness in us is to deny that God, who is goodness itself, is our Creator. So we need to ask ourselves what blocks us from accepting our innate goodness? The mark of our true greatness and potential is that we are made in the image and likeness of God.

Our poor self-image is an aspect of our sinfulness, which is always with us. Within us there is always this struggle between our innate goodness, which aspires to God, and our sinfulness, which seeks to satisfy ourselves.

The Christian basis for a healthy self-image is the dignity that belongs to us because we have been created by God. We are all God's children, members of God's Christian family. We were created in God's image (Genesis 1:26–27).

Reflection: Our Deepest Fear

Realising that you are a child of God, and therefore unique, powerful and talented, can be more frightening than continuing with your low self-image. Can you take the risk of starting to see yourself as a child of God? It will be worth it.

Many people got into heavy drinking and other drugs because they felt inadequate. For some it was issues about their appearance or not excelling in school, or wanting to be popular with their peer group and failing. For young men it is often around their sexual performance, which they feel is inadequate. It can also be peer pressure, social expectations, boredom, feeling inadequate as friends, parents and partners or workers.

Self-respect means knowing that we are worth something, knowing our own dignity, value and especially our uniqueness as a person. God wants us to be integrated, whole people, fruitful and productive and full of new ideas.

Thomas Aquinas taught that every one of us is a unique expression of God in this world. I therefore have to discover the unique image of God that I am and discover and understand the mystery of my own existence. When I begin to discover my own uniqueness, I will then begin to stop comparing myself to others, stop taking my lead from other people's expectations of me. I will begin to be myself and discover my own inner resources and self-worth.

When you come to realise that you are worth something, then you will be able to treat your body, mind and soul with respect and stop abusing them with addictive substances and behaviours.

Self-respect doesn't mean that I will always appear self-assured. It is about accepting myself flaws and all.

We are a long way on the journey when we are able to accept our shadow side and become reconciled with our life history. A healthy image of myself is one that accepts the light and dark aspects of myself, the good and the bad, the divine and the human.

There comes a point when looking back on my life is no longer fruitful. At some point we have to take responsibility for our own life. We have to accept our past as a learning curve for the task before us now and decide to shape our own life for the future.

Once we begin to take responsibility for our own life, we stop blaming other people or situations for our own bad luck or suffering. Instead we open our eyes to the opportunities available to us *now*. We begin to become aware of the unique image that God has produced in us and that God wants to be born in us in a unique way.

How do we do this?

Start by discarding the various false identities that we have surrounded ourselves with. For example:

- Do I define myself by my parents' opinions, or the opinions of my brothers or sisters, or those of my peer group?
- Do I define myself in terms of success and achievement, or money and power?
- Do I define myself with what I see on Instagram or Facebook, or in magazines such as *Hello*, or TV, and when I cannot achieve that image do I feel like a failure?

Note the AA daily examination asks, 'Are we still trying to be people pleasers in order to gain approval from other people even at the expense of our own dignity and self-respect?'

As long as we identify ourselves with external sources we remain dependent on them and blind to our true authentic selves. We have to stop looking for our self-evaluation in the acceptance or confirmation of others and seek it within ourselves in the loving gaze of God.

My true self is more than the sum of all that has happened to me: more than my drinking, my drug taking, my gambling, my sexual encounters, my upbringing, my education, my work, my life history. My true self is a mystery because it is where God expresses God's own self in a unique way.

Concluding Prayer: The Our Father

Reminder
- Keep reflecting on 'my purpose in life' and keep practising the daily Examen and daily prayer.
- Keep listening for God's question, 'What do you want?'
- Keep in mind that you are a loved sinner.
- Do you need to walk down a different street?
- What do you need healing from?
- Can you see that in your deepest self you are really like God, because that is the way that God made you?

The Passion and Death of Jesus

The Passion

The Passion and death of Jesus is in all four Gospels (Matthew 26:36–27:50; Mark 14:32–15:39; Luke 22:39–24:46; John 18–19:30). Take any of these gospels and read the story for yourselves.

Remember when we started out on this journey, we told you (Reflection 2) about how Jesus, when he lived on this earth, preached a message of good news. The leaders of his time, both political and religious, did not like his message, as it challenged the way they lived and what they taught. Failing to silence him, they decided to get rid of him, and with the support of the people he was sentenced to death on a cross.

Before his arrest Jesus celebrated the Last Supper with his disciples, one of whom – Judas Iscariot – was about to betray him. During his life Jesus had told the people that 'unless you eat my body and drink my blood, you cannot have eternal life'. By this he meant that you had to follow him to the end if you want to be his disciple.

At that Last Supper, Jesus blessed bread and wine and gave them to his disciples, saying, 'This is my body. This is my blood. Do this in memory of me.' This is what Christians receive when they participate in communion.

After this Last Supper, he went with his disciples to a garden outside Jerusalem called Gethsemane. He left the disciples in a group and went a little apart to pray.

Here he experienced great anxiety and fear.

This might seem strange because he is the Son of God, but Jesus was also fully human, and as a human being he was terrified in the face of death.

He was not stupid. He knew what faced people who challenged the religious and political powers. That is why he took so long before deciding to 'set his face to go to Jerusalem' (Luke 9:51). He knew that his greatest enemies were in the city.

In the garden, not only did he face the fear of death, but he also saw the complete collapse of all his dreams: his hopes for a new world of peace and respect.

Even though he was the Son of God, he was faced with temptations and fear like we are. But through his suffering he learned faithfulness and obedience to the Father right to the end.

What about his disciples, those he had called to follow him and who had been with him for three years? They all fell asleep! It seemed as if his whole life was a disaster, and all that faced him was the agony of crucifixion and failure.

He said, 'My soul is deeply grieved, even to death' (Matthew 26:38–40). He prayed that, if it were possible, 'let this cup pass from me, yet not what I want but what you want' (Matthew 26:38–40). He was in such agony that his sweat became like drops of blood falling on the ground (Luke 22:44). Eventually he was consoled by an angel from heaven.

He got up and went back to the sleeping disciples. He said to Peter, 'So, could you not stay awake with me one hour?' Then he said something very important for all of us, 'Stay awake and pray that you may not come into the time of trial; the spirit indeed is willing, but the flesh is weak' (Matthew 26:40–41).

At that point the soldiers arrived, led by Judas, one of his closest friends who now betrayed him. Judas had told the soldiers, who did not know Jesus, that he would point him out by going up to Jesus and kissing him. Then the soldiers grabbed Jesus and hauled him off to jail. He spent that night in prison.

He was brought before four courts: first the religious court, then the court of Herod, the local king, then before the religious court again, and finally before the court of Pilate, the local governor.

It was not a fair trial. He had no barrister. The witnesses lied. The prosecution kept changing the charges. He was found guilty, even though he was innocent.

The sentence was death, by crucifixion.

Before being crucified he was scourged and beaten by two soldiers with a whip until he bled. At the end of each cord were tied sharp pieces of bone. Then he was made carry his cross through the streets, while the people jeered and laughed at him.

When they got to Calvary, they nailed him to the cross.

They stuck a notice on the Cross that said, 'Jesus of Nazareth, King of the Jews'. This was to humiliate him and served as a warning so that everyone else would know what would happen to them if they got out of line.

Hanging each side of him were two prisoners guilty of crimes. One confessed. Immediately Jesus turned to him and forgave him, saying, 'This day you will be with me in Paradise.' The other chose not to. God gives us this freedom to choose.

Jesus prayed for those torturing him, 'Father, forgive them, for they know not what they are doing.'

Before he died he cried out in agony, 'My God, my God, why have you forsaken me?' He looked for a miracle from his Father, his Abba (Daddy), and no miracle came.

Yet, despite this, Our Lord kept trusting and believing in his Abba. His last words were, 'Father, into thy hands I commend my spirit.'

Reflection on the Passion of Jesus

What strikes you as you read and listen to this story? What feelings do you have? Do you find any connection between this story and your own life? Maybe ask yourself some of the following questions.

- Have you ever felt despair?
- Were you ever tempted to give it all up? Did you ever feel that life was too awful, that you would rather be dead?
- Have you ever been terrified?
- Did you ever feel abandoned by everyone?
- Were you ever beaten up?
- Were you ever hauled before a court?

- Did you ever feel you got a raw deal, or had to take the rap for someone else?
- Did you ever find yourself in a mess, and there seemed to be no way out?

The really important point about Jesus is that he shows us what God is like. Jesus is the image of God in our world. If you want to know God, then look at him. What do you see? Someone who:

- really loved people,
- had huge compassion for people when they were in trouble,
- wanted to bring healing to all those who were suffering,
- would not separate himself from sinners. Indeed, he preferred hanging around with them than with those who thought they were better than everyone else,
- who trusted in his God right to the end, even in the darkness of the cross,
- who forgave the thief who was crucified with him and forgave his own torturers.

Jesus was trying to show us something else about God. We hear it a lot, but we don't take it in: God *really* loves you and me.

Look at the following quotes from the scriptures:

- 'For God so loved the world that he gave his only Son, that whoever believes in him may not perish but have eternal life' (John 3:16).
- 'In this is love, not that we loved God but that he loved us and sent his Son to be the atoning sacrifice for our sins' (1 John 4:10).
- 'But God proves his love for us in that while we were still sinners Christ died for us' (Romans 5:8).
- 'I will never leave you or forsake you' (Hebrews 13:5–6).

How much of this do you believe? How often have you experienced God's love? Do you still think you have to be good for God to love you? (Of course we have to be good, but that comes *after* we realise that God loves us). How much does God need to do to get this across to you? Why will you not listen to God when he tells you how much he cares for you?

We are told that after he died on the cross, Jesus descended into hell. What does this mean? It means that no one damned by the world is beyond the reach of our loving God. It means God never gives up on any of us. God loves us so much that he just can't do that, even when everyone else has given up or we ourselves have given up. No matter what situation we have got ourselves into, God is there with us.

We can be confident that if we turn to God that we will be made incredibly welcome.

The cross looked like the end for Jesus, but it was not. On the contrary it was the greatest moment of his life. John's Gospel talks about the cross as being the 'hour' of Jesus. It was for this that he came into the world: to show us that there were no lengths to which God would not go to reach out to us.

On the cross one human being, one of *us*, lived his life to the full. He showed that it is possible for us to be fully human, fully alive, fully faithful, despite the mess we make of things. He did this on behalf of all of us. He invites us to enter into his world, to start living our lives to the full, to become fully alive, to be faithful to God, to ourselves and to all others in our world.

That may seem like a big task, but we are not asked to do it on our own. Jesus is with us. And 'if God is for us, who can be against us?' (Romans: 8:31).

Pope Francis, leading the Way of the Cross, 10 April 2020, said:

> Accompanying Christ on the Way of the Cross, with the raw voices of those who live behind the walls of a prison, is an opportunity to view the great battle between life and death, to discover how the threads of good and evil intertwine. Contemplating Calvary from behind bars is to believe that an entire life can be played out in a few moments, as happened to the good thief.

All it takes is to fill those moments with truth: contrition for sins committed, the realisation that death is not for ever, the certainty that Christ is the innocent man unjustly mocked. Everything is possible for those who believe, because even in the darkness of prison there resounds the proclamation full of hope: 'For with God nothing is impossible' (Luke 1:37).

If someone holds out to them a hand, those capable of the most horrendous crimes can undergo the most unexpected resurrection. We can be certain that 'even when we tell of evil, we can learn to leave room for redemption; in the midst of evil, we can also recognise the working of goodness and give it space'.

Closing Prayer: The Our Father

Reminder
- Keep reflecting on 'my purpose in life' and keep practising the daily Examen and daily prayer.
- Keep listening for God's question, 'What do you want?'
- Keep in mind that you are a loved sinner.
- Do you need to walk down a different street?
- What do you need healing from?
- Can you see that in your deepest self you are really like God, because that is the way that God made you?
- Jesus suffered and died out of love for *you*.

The Call of the King

At Our Baptism We Were Called to Follow Jesus

Few of us remember the day we were baptised. Our parents or carers probably brought us along to the church at some point when we were babies or still very small. Maybe some of you have done the same for your own children.

For those of us baptised as babies, our baptism was the moment when we were chosen by God to become members of God's Christian family – what we call the Church. (It also has the same meaning if we were baptised as adults, but we likely remember it!) We were given a name, which is the name God knows us by, because each one of us is unique in the eyes of God. In prison you are given a number and that number stays with you all the time you are in prison. Outside of prison people often feel they are just a number where they work, but for God you are not just a number, you are called by your name.

At baptism your parents, sponsors and the community made a commitment on your behalf to bring you up in the Christian faith and that requires us to live by the laws and values laid down for Christian living.

As baptised Christians we all have a contribution to make to the spiritual well-being of the Church family of which we are members.

As baptised Christians we have two families. There is the family we all recognise, in which we may have mothers, fathers, grandparents, brothers, sisters, uncles, aunts and cousins, and there is a much bigger family. This is God's family. God is our Father, and everyone in the world is our brother and sister. In this family we are all unique and equal in God's eyes irrespective of class, colour, gender or creed. God our Father loves us all and asks us to love each other.

Let's remind ourselves what the 'Principle and Foundation' ('My purpose in life', Reflection 1) tells us:

We are created to praise, reverence and serve God our Lord, and by this means to save our soul.

All other things on the face of the earth are created for us to help us reach this goal.

We are to use all other things in as much as they help us to achieve this goal, and to refrain from using those things in so far as they are a hindrance.

Therefore, with respect to all created things in which we have a free choice, it is necessary to become detached.

Consequently, on our part, we should not prefer health to sickness, riches to poverty, a long life to a short one, honour to dishonour and so for all things our one desire and choice should be what is most conducive for the goal for which we are created.

In the above Ignatius tells us what he means by freedom and what our ultimate purpose in life is, to live with God forever.

Out of love we were called into life; out of love we were called from death through sin; out of love we are constantly being called into trusting what real life can be with and alongside Jesus.

His call to us is a freedom *from* something and a freedom *to* something. We should now know what bad parts of our life we are being called to leave behind. We should also know what we are being called to, even though we may be afraid of this, and therefore need to pray more about it. This is the call of our baptism into Jesus. How special we are to receive such an invitation of love!

We can all admit that too often in the past we have been too busy or too drunk to hear the call, let alone respond to it. Now that we have experienced the forgiving and healing love of God, we can hear this call as love's invitation.

How Do We Respond to the Call of Jesus?

The question for us is how do we respond to this invitation. When a loved one calls us, we will normally say, 'yes', even if the cost of what he or she asks is great. We say 'yes' because we want to be with the person we love.

Jesus is calling us to join him in building up this new community that he wants to see in our world. The call will be different for everyone. We all have different gifts. We have different experiences and a different history that has shaped our unique ability to be compassionate and responsive.

Many of us respond 'yes' when we discover that there is no real happiness in life that doesn't involve following Jesus.

What will be important is the depth of our response, how completely we respond.

Maybe we could begin by saying that when we make choices or decisions in future we will always ask: will this bring me to do what God wants me to do? If I keep taking alcohol and other drugs will this bring me to what God wants?

Most of us want a long life and good health and wealth, but Ignatius tells us we must remain detached from such desires, otherwise they may become the dominant force in our lives.

So we are invited to look at the areas that often take our focus away from God as the centre of our life. Hence, as we live our lives each day, we should become more aware that the choices and decisions we make are important. This requires reflecting on the consequences of our actions before we act or before we speak. It requires greater reliance on God through prayer. Then we make the better choice, which is ultimately to serve God.

Freedom is one of the most important gifts for us if we are to grow at a human and spiritual level. By clinging to anything, we create a lack of freedom in ourselves that limits us.

For example, if I cling to the belief that I have been unjustly treated, that the other is in the wrong and has made me angry, and that I was justified in beating him up, then I soon become stuck, and I am no longer as free as I could be. If I cling to the idea that I'm not as good as everyone else, then I am stuck and no longer free.

God has given each of us the gift of life because he loves us. Each response of love allows God's life to flow into us. Everything in this world is gift, created for us so that we can know God better, love him more deeply and serve him more faithfully. Ignatius encourages us to use all our gifts and even creation itself to attain this goal.

We exist for God. We live for God. We therefore must respond to things, people and situations in a way that praises God and expresses our love for him. In John 14:23 Jesus says: 'If anyone loves me, they will keep my word and my Father will love them and we will come to them and make our home with them.'

Jesus came among us to bring about the kingdom of God here on earth. He always knew that he would need followers to come after him who would bring his message of love and peace to others. We are those followers.

By our baptism we are called to witness to Christ by how we live our Christian lives. We all exist for God. We are called to be fully human, called to be in Christ Jesus, called to serve him and to help him build up the kingdom in some particular way.

To do this inner freedom is necessary. This call presumes that I am free to hear the call, free to respond to it and that I have the power and strength to carry it out. Such freedom is beyond my own achievement. It is God's gift to each of us, and we should pray for this gift. Then we will be free from all those doubts and negative thoughts that make us deaf to his call.

This inner freedom is only possible when we desire it. My only desire and my only choice should be to want and to choose what best leads me to God deepening his life in me.

Today God needs your hands, your feet, your eyes, your words to carry his love to the people around you. That can be as simple as offering a word of encouragement to someone in trouble. It can mean walking away from some temptation that you know to be wrong. It may be walking away from those who were your friends or drinking buddies, because they are a cause of temptation for you.

How Can I Use My Gifts?

Focus for a moment on the gifts and talents that God has given you.

- Do I recognise my own talents?
- Do I realise that these talents are God's gift to me?
- Do I thank God for the talents he has given me?

God gave me the gift of life and the ability to use the physical, mental and spiritual gifts that I have. Do I recognise these as gifts from God showing me how much he loves me? How would I like to use these gifts in future to show my appreciation to God?

All of us can do more to educate and train ourselves, and thereby to develop the gifts God has given us. We can learn to read, to write, to build, to paint, to cook, to garden, to fix bicycles, to make ceramics, to sing and to pray. The list is endless. Each of us has a call to develop our gifts.

Ignatius encourages us to use everything at our disposal to attain our goal, which is to serve and love God. Look at the talents you have and see how you can use these for this goal.

Jesus tells us that until we are living in a relationship with God we will never find true meaning and purpose in our life. Other things might provide passing satisfaction, like wild living and parties, but as the prodigal son found out to his cost these don't last. Only in a relationship with God, our Creator, will we find true meaning and purpose in our lives.

Remember at the start of these reflections we found that Ignatius also discovered this. Read his story again (Reflection 1).

St Paul tells us:

> For you were called to freedom, brothers and sisters, only do not use your freedom as an opportunity for self-indulgence ...

the works of the flesh are obvious: sexual immorality, impurity, debauchery, idolatry, sorcery, enmities, strife, jealousy, anger, quarrels, dissensions, factions, envy, drunkenness, carousing, and things like these. (Galatians: 5:13–21)

The idea of gift is at the heart of the Christian mystery. All that we are and all that we have comes from God. His first gift to each of us is his eternal and everlasting love. (Go back to the story of the prodigal father in Reflection 4). From that flows the gift of creation, when he gave us the gift of life, the potential to grow as full human beings who are children of God.

To this end God gave us the gift of all creatures, especially people, with whom we can grow and praise God. God gave us himself as the Creator, Saviour, Sanctifier whom we worship. The Father is constantly drawing human beings to himself through adoration and love. He continues to make us in his own image and likeness.

Our personal experience of life is a most precious gift. It is unique, it is me, yet also much more than me. It is God in me, with me, acting through me. So I need to keep the focus on God.

Jesus used all his humanity: his mind, his heart, his will, his senses, everything, to know himself and to know his Father. Through these gifts he experienced life. Do you do the same?

Misappropriation, or abuse of the gift, lies at the heart of sin. We do this when we refuse to acknowledge that everything we are and have comes from God. That we have nothing of ourselves, only what God has given us. When we accept this truth then we want to worship God and surrender to him.

When we claim gifts as our own, we might hope to be independent and gloat in a distorted self-esteem. We become like the younger son in the story of the prodigal before his conversion. This is idolatry of ourselves, and it is a sin. So if someone is glorifying in their own success pray for them rather than feeling inferior to them.

All that I am and all that I have is God's gift of love to me.

God himself is present in each gift of love to me.

How do I know where I am meant to be serving and what I am supposed to be doing?

One way to discover the answer is to ask God to show you the gifts that you have. Many people do not find it easy to name these, but because each of us is different, each of us has gifts that no one else has. We have to search to find out what these gifts are. We do this through prayer, through listening to the deepest desires within ourselves and through asking other people. Think of the question we asked at the beginning of these reflections: what is it that you really want?

God's Holy Spirit pours into us the gifts and talents that are the tools we need for the task to which God calls us.

Some of the different gifts people have include: being a father or mother, looking after a sick parent or grandparent, delving into the truth of our faith, developing our musical talents, singing in God's service, helping out in charity shops or other organisations that help the poor and the needy, treating the environment with respect and reverence, and just the ordinary love in ordinary days in the family, in sharing love and in care for others.

You don't need a university degree to help others. It takes some talent to work out how to break into a house or shop or bank to steal money to feed your addiction. So how about using your talents to help others and to help God build his kingdom here on earth? Nothing is wasted in what we can do for God. God wants us to use the gifts he gave us to build up his kingdom (1 Corinthians 12:4–11).

God gives us life because he loves us. When I respond with love God's life flows into me without limit. Everything in this world is a gift of God, created for us so that we can know, love and serve him more deeply. As a result, I appreciate and use all these gifts of God in so far as they help me to develop as a loving person, but if any of these gifts become the centre of my life, they displace God and so hinder my growth towards my goal. God calls us into freedom.

Inner freedom cannot be achieved by my own efforts. It is a gift of God. Pray for the gift of that inner freedom.

Do You Think That Your Life and You Yourself Are a Gift?

When we consider that Jesus, who is the Son of God, chose to become a human being as we are, except for sin, we begin to appreciate more the goodness that is at the very centre of us human beings. Unless we value highly the richness, dignity and potential of others as God intends the peak of creation to be, how can we grasp the kind of love which God the Creator has for us? He intended us to be 'little less than a god'.

Unless we believe in the goodness of our visible humanity, we will find it difficult to believe in that which is beyond our human experience and not yet visible, namely, that we are children of God and co-heirs with Christ.

Closing Prayer: The Our Father

Remember
- Keep reflecting on 'my purpose in life' and keep practising the daily Examen and daily prayer.
- Keep listening for God's question, 'What do you want?'
- Keep in mind that you are a loved sinner.
- Do you need to walk down a different street?
- What do you need healing from?
- Can you see that in your deepest self you are really like God, because that is the way that God made you?
- Jesus suffered and died out of love for you.
- Are you open to hearing what God is calling you to?

Reflection 9:

Saying Yes to God: The Response of Mary

In our last reflection we looked at the call of the kingdom. In this reflection we will look at the call of Mary, the Mother of God, and how she responded to God's call.

Mary's Call

We will start by reading Luke 1:26–38.

> In the sixth month the angel Gabriel was sent by God to a town in Galilee called Nazareth, to a virgin engaged to a man whose name was Joseph, of the house of David. The virgin's name was Mary. And he came to her and said, 'Greetings, favoured one! The Lord is with you.' But she was much perplexed by his words and pondered what sort of greeting this might be. The angel said to her, 'Do not be afraid, Mary, for you have found favour with God. And now, you will conceive in your womb and bear a son, and you will name him Jesus. He will be great and will be called the Son of the Most High, and the Lord God will give to him the throne of his ancestor David. He will reign over the house of Jacob forever, and of his kingdom there will be no end.' Mary said to the angel, 'How can this be, since I am a virgin?' The angel said to her, 'The Holy Spirit will come upon you, and the power of the Most High will overshadow you; therefore the child to be born will be holy; he will be called Son of God. And now, your relative Elizabeth in her old age has also conceived a son, and this is the sixth month for her who was said to be barren. For nothing will be impossible with God.' Then Mary said,

'Here am I, the servant of the Lord; let it be with me according to your word.' Then the angel departed from her.

Mary obviously spent a lot of time in prayer, and it was during one of these prayer times that God asked her to be the mother of his Son. Not surprisingly, we are told that Mary was troubled at this message. She was a very young girl at the time, human in every way.

Suddenly, God calls her to something profound – to give birth to his Son. She must have been totally bewildered and puzzled by this, and not fully understanding what was going on. We are told in the above reading that Mary was troubled by the request. Despite her troubled feelings, she did not run away or hide, but remained present to the experience she was having, to the call of God, to something immense.

What does she do? We are told that she ponders what this greeting of God's messenger could mean. She tries to understand the significance of the message. Can you imagine what that was like for her? She probably spent more time in prayer, listening, wondering and discerning.

Finally, she says yes to God, 'Let it be with me according to your word.'

Mary was called to be the mother of the Messiah. This was a spiritual experience between herself and God that took place in the very depths of her being.

Mary was a fully human young girl when faced with this challenge and decision, but what it shows is that she was truly a young person of faith.

With Mary's yes to God's call, God enters our world in a new way, in a human way. He knocks at Mary's door. He waits on human freedom. The only way he can redeem humankind, who have been created free, is by a free 'yes' to God's will and Mary provides that 'yes'.

In the end we are told that the angel departed from her, so she is left alone with the task which surpasses all human tasks. She must continue along the journey of life. This will lead to many dark moments right up to the foot of the cross. We are all called to make that journey, a journey with many ups and downs. There will be times when, like Mary, we too will be puzzled and bewildered. When we experience that confusion we must stick with it, keep going, remain steadfast, knowing that God journeys with us all the way, while we are learning to trust him.

Mary's Response to Her Call

If we look back at the scene on Calvary as Jesus was dying on the cross, we find Mary at the foot of the cross with St John. Jesus as he was dying said to her, 'Woman, behold your son' and to St John he said, 'Son behold your mother'. As Jesus was dying on the cross Mary was standing with him, suffering with him, and she became the mother of all Christians, our mother.

Prayer to Mary our mother is part of our Christian heritage. In the Litany of Our Lady we call her 'Refuge of Sinners', a mother's heart always forgiving, 'Comforter of the Afflicted'. A mother knows how to be gentle and tender.

Mary encourages us to persevere with the journey that is set before us. She is not the only witness to this. Other witnesses may include your own mother or grandmother or other loved ones. Their lives may not always have been perfect, yet with their faults and failings, their ups and downs, they kept going forward and proved pleasing to the Lord in doing so.

Through Mary's 'yes' her whole life changed. Like any mother she was still needed by her Son, but through her yes she welcomed God into her life. Mary was tested throughout her life, but like Jesus she remained faithful.

Through your 'yes', your life too can be changed.

Questions
- How often do we stick with difficult moments that come up in our prayer and try to understand them?
- What distracts you in your prayer?

- Mary shows us that every parent will have good and difficult moments in raising their children. Can you bring your difficulties to Mary in prayer?
- When you think of God calling you to give up alcohol and other drugs, do you feel troubled? Can you stick with that pain, or do you run away in fear?
- Can you turn to Mary for encouragement?
- Like her, with total trust in God, can you say: Yes, let it be done to me according to your word?

For many, prayer to Our Lady is important. Most of you will know the prayer of the Rosary, and this can be a wonderful way to start praying to Mary. In the prison where I ran some prayer sessions, I noticed many wore rosary beads around their necks. How about taking the rosary beads from around your necks and starting to pray the rosary, as through it we get familiar with the full journey of Jesus and Mary?

- In the Joyful Mysteries we pray over the call of Mary and the birth of Jesus and his early years.
- In the Mysteries of Light, we pray over the mission of Jesus.
- In the Sorrowful Mysteries, we pray over the passion and death of Jesus.
- In the Glorious mysteries we pray over the Resurrection of Jesus from the dead and the sending down to us of the Holy Spirit who guides and directs us with our daily choices and decisions.

It's all there in a nutshell. Make the Rosary a regular prayer.

Closing Prayer: The Hail Mary

Reminder
- Keep reflecting on 'my purpose in life' and keep practising the daily Examen and daily prayer.
- Keep listening for God's question, 'What do you want?'

- Keep in mind that you are a loved sinner.
- Do you need to walk down a different street?
- What do you need healing from?
- Can you see that in your deepest self you are really like God, because that is the way that God made you?
- Jesus suffered and died out of love for you.
- Are you open to hear what God is calling you to?
- Can you take inspiration from the example of Mary when you need courage and help?

Temptations

- What are your greatest temptations?
- What is going on inside you when you feel tempted?
- Who are you thinking of most when being tempted?

It doesn't matter whether it's the temptation for more alcohol or other drugs, or to make more money, or to have more power. What's important is to notice that there is a battle going on inside you between two things that you desire.

Many people use different ways to describe this battle. Ignatius talks of the good and bad spirit, Carl Jung of the shadow and the light inside us. Whatever phrase we use, we can all recognise that we have a battle on our hands between two sides of ourselves. In this section I will talk of our spiritual side and our shadow side.

Christians believe that the spirit of Jesus helps us to get in touch with our spiritual side and also that the bad spirit, or our selfishness, which is influenced by communal selfishness, draws us down into our shadow side.

Selfishness and self-centredness can be at work in your shadow side. At the same time you know in your spiritual self that what you desire is to fulfil your own selfish needs not what your spiritual self, deep down, wants. And so the battle goes on.

How Does the Shadow Side of You Operate?

Let's say that you decide to give up alcohol or other drugs, or whatever is having a negative effect on your life. You decide to turn over a new leaf, to live a better life and to seek God's help.

Your shadow side wants the opposite for you. It throws up all the difficulties and problems you will have in living a life of sobriety. It will attempt to rouse a false sadness in you for what you are going to miss. It will tempt you to change the rules or to start blaming others. It will give you a false anxiety about persevering.

It will suggest innumerable roadblocks, discouragement and deception, in your effort to walk or live the way the Lord wishes you to. It will use your best friends to tempt you too.

It will convince you to keep playing the games that you have got used to, the denial and the lies that have worked for so long. It will whisper in your ear: 'Why give them up since they did no harm to anyone?'

Your shadow self will tell you that:

- The job you lost wasn't worth having in the first place.
- The wife who walked out on you was never any use. You should never have married her in the first place.
- The kids never bothered with you, and their mother turned them away from you.
- With the alcohol and other drugs, you don't have any of these problems in my way.
- You're much happier now that you've got away from them all.
- You were just unlucky that you got caught and ended up in prison, or that your family turned against you: what would they know anyway?
- If you're smarter the next time you can avoid prison, because a lot of your friends outside take alcohol and other drugs and don't get caught. You just have to be more careful in future.

The shadow side will help you to believe any and all of these messages, that drugs are doing you no harm and that you don't have a problem. It is everyone else who has a problem, not you. Above all it will have you believe that you are not addicted.

Getting in touch with your spiritual side, on the other hand, will strengthen and encourage you, console and inspire you to do what is right. It will help you to see the reality of your life, what your addictions have done to you physically, mentally and emotionally, and how unhappy you really are behind the facades you have learned to maintain.

With the help of your spiritual side, you will eventually let down the false masks, stop lying and face that war between the two sides of yourself.

Responding to Temptations

Recovery and the spiritual path are about reclaiming our true nature: I am a child of God made in his image and likeness.

This will be difficult at first, but if you persevere you will, in time, find joy and peace. You will be better able to deal with daily living. With God's grace you will be able to face the obstacles that come your way. The spiritual side thereby continues an upright person's progress in responding to God's continuing invitation.

The spiritual side works in different ways for everyone. It might be through your friends or your family. It could be through a spiritual guide, or it might be through counselling, or AA, or NA, or through your own personal prayer.

The Twelve-Step Programme in AA offers an inspired spiritual practice to anyone who chooses to use it. The programme has proved its effectiveness since it first started in 1935 and millions of people have benefited from it, but as we see from the temptations this will involve a constant struggle between our spiritual and shadow sides. This struggle will continue for all of us for all our lives. What we have to do is to live out of the spiritual side and deal with the shadow side. That requires constant prayer and trust in God's grace which is freely available to us. In the Twelve-Step Programme it means attending to our struggle each day and putting our trust in a higher power.

Ignatius in the Spiritual Exercises talks about Discernment of Spirits, the basis of which is the fact that temptations are commonly encountered on the spiritual path.

True consolation comes, he says, from the Good Spirit. Desolation from the bad spirit. He says the best protection against our shadow side is to open our heart to someone we trust. He notes:

> the enemy also acts like a false lover, who wishes to be hidden and does not want to be known … When the enemy of our human nature tempts a just soul with his tricks and deceits he wants and desires that they be kept secret. When they are revealed to a confessor or some other spiritual person who understands his deceipts and malicious designs, the enemy is greatly displeased for he knows that he cannot win in his evil plan once his obvious deceits have been laid bare.

When I know and am able to deal with my spiritual and shadow sides, I will be whole at last. Self-control, self-discipline and sobriety are linked to prayer for the Christian and are its essential prerequisites. Prayer is not an activity of the mind, for God is not in the head, but rather an activity of the whole person.

In his Gospel, St John keeps repeating how darkness fights against light, the liar against truth, death against life.

Jesus himself speaks plainly about two forces within us, leading us to freedom or to destruction. The destructive side demands that we get some alcohol or other drug, or give into whatever is our addiction. The good news is that the liberating force is much, much stronger (and gentler), even though the dark force shouts louder. Jesus calls us to a freedom that is the very opposite of our addiction which is a captivating, dominating force that is both external to us and yet embedded within us.

Your shadow side wants to wrap all other people around yourself, to serve your selfish needs. People dominated by darkness want others to share their darkness. Birds of a feather flock together. It is like the corona virus: highly contagious. The drug dealer sucks you in.

The Temptations of Jesus

One consolation for all of us is that whatever temptations we experience Jesus knows exactly what that feels like. Go back to Reflection 2 and read again how Jesus became human and suffered everything that we might experience, and much more, when he lived on this earth. He knows what temptations are like, he has been there, so we should be able to talk freely to him about our struggles. We are told in the Gospels:

> And when Jesus had been baptised, just as he came up from the water, suddenly the heavens were opened to him and he saw God's Spirit descending like a dove and alighting on him. And a voice from the heavens said, 'This is my Son, the Beloved, with whom I am well pleased.' (Matthew 3:16–17)

> Then Jesus was led up by the Spirit into the wilderness to be tested by the devil. He fasted forty days and forty nights, and afterward he was famished. (See Matthew 4:1–11)

Here we see Jesus himself wrestling with temptation. What is clear from the story is that Jesus does not either give into or run away from his temptation.

In this story he is facing up to who he is: 'My Beloved Son', God's Son. In other words, he is keeping in touch with his deepest identity. A lot of power went with that identity that could be used in the wrong way. He could have decided to use this power for himself rather than for others. This is what our dark side wants us to do.

In the gospel story Jesus has been fasting and praying. He is very hungry and thirsty. So Satan first uses this temptation. Satan always goes after our weak spots. He says to Jesus, 'If you are the Son of God command these stones to become loaves of bread'. This is very tempting if you're hungry. What does Jesus say? 'Man does not live by bread alone, but by every word that comes from the mouth of God.' He refuses to give in to the desire for power. He knows he must depend on God's power.

Freedom is all about facing up to the temptation to use our power for our own gratification. Self-gratification turns inwards, gets smaller and smaller, and less and less satisfying. Using what we have to help others, that is a path that widens and deepens and grows. The dark side always focuses on *our* hungers, *our* thirsts, *our* needs and gratifications whatever they may be. Those in any kind of addiction will know what they are. But there are many hungers: for money, success, power, prestige, sex, to be liked, to be the centre of attention, etc. Grabbing on to the truth that all our needs are met in relation to other people is the way towards the light, and it is the way that Jesus followed in the desert.

Jesus knew his own temptations. He turned away from them and chose to give himself to whatever God desired. Then he could joyfully accept unpopularity and being rejected, if that helped him to help others. This is the spiritual force at work.

Many people, not just people in addiction, are unaware of their spiritual potential or actively attempt to disown that part of themselves. When we deny or repress this drive it is often because we fear the change it might require us to make and this often means, for those in addiction, having to lose control. Fear is at the root of compulsive behaviour, i.e. fear of becoming conscious of reality.

We may have to confront new and difficult aspects of ourselves, and this can be very frightening, so we deny the existence of this aspect of our self and defend our stance at any cost. But none of us are perfect, we are a flawed human race. There are difficult aspects of ourselves to be faced on this journey to recovery and they have to be integrated into our journey. It is a journey or a process that lasts a lifetime.

To truly reach a place of wholeness, we have to love ourselves, to forgive ourselves, to accept the inevitable pain of the human condition, and to endure it to reach a higher goal.

Unfortunately, in our addiction, the bottle or drug becomes our best friend. While it might be described as a love relationship, it is focused on a need to escape from feelings of powerlessness and insecurity in my darker side.

If we connect with the spiritual side of ourselves, where there is a power greater than ourselves; if we surrender ourselves, accept ourselves and open ourselves to our human vulnerability, then we connect with the deeper part of ourselves.

This opens us to true intimacy. This is an intimacy of inner acceptance, softness and tenderness with ourselves and an intimacy of mutual exchange of our vulnerability.

I am like the prodigal son: a sinner.

Like the prodigal son, despite my sinfulness, I am loved by God.

These qualities do not develop all at once. It takes time and courage, patience, willingness and a great deal of attention to connect to our deeper selves. Connecting with our higher power is crucial to help us to do this.

Within the Twelve-Step Programme, the higher power is as you understand it. It can mean your core inner self or your creative energy, the force of love, the mystery of life, compassion and nurturing that comes from another person, or the group of people walking the walk with you and who care.

Others see it as representing our potential, the unlimited possibilities and gifts that may lie hidden within us. Others describe it as the Great Spirit, the Beloved within, our source of inspiration, our God. It can mean Allah or Jesus of Nazareth. We should never allow others to impose their beliefs on us, but we can tap into our own and other traditions and faiths to deepen our own wisdom.

What is important to understand is that, irrespective of how we describe it or experience it, this spiritual drive or force lies within each of us, and we can tap into it. Thousands who were in addiction are living witnesses to this.

The Twelve Promises of AA

1. We are going to know a new freedom and a new happiness.
2. We will not regret the past or wish to shut the door on it.
3. We will comprehend the word serenity and we will know peace.
4. No matter how far down the scale we have gone, we will see how our experience can benefit others.
5. The feelings of uselessness and self-pity will disappear.
6. We will lose interest in selfish things and gain interest in our fellows.
7. Self-seeking will slip away.

8. Our whole attitude and outlook upon life will change.
9. Fear of people and of economic insecurity will leave us.
10. We will intuitively know how to handle situations which used to baffle us.
11. We will suddenly realise that God is doing for us what we could not do for ourselves.
12. Are these extravagant promises? We think not. They are being fulfilled among us, sometimes quickly, sometimes slowly. They will always materialise if we work for them.

Closing Prayer: The Our Father

Reminder
- Keep reflecting on 'my purpose in life' and keep practising the daily Examen and daily prayer.
- Keep listening for God's question, 'What do you want?'
- Keep in mind that you are a loved sinner.
- Do you need to walk down a different street?
- What do you need healing from?
- Can you see that in your deepest self you are really like God, because that is the way that God made you?
- Jesus suffered and died out of love for you.
- Are you open to hear what God is calling you to?
- Can you take inspiration from the example of Mary when you need courage and help?
- Can you keep begging for the grace of light to illumine your darkness?

Reflection 11:

The Resurrection of Jesus

All four Gospels, Matthew, Mark, Luke and John, describe meetings between the disciples and Our Lord after his resurrection. These meetings feature several themes:

- The disciples always refuse to believe when others tell them that they have met the Risen Christ.
- When Jesus appears they often do not recognise him.
- At first they are filled with fear.
- Jesus always blesses them with peace.

Almost all the disciples fled after the crucifixion and locked themselves into a safe place as they were frightened for their lives. Interestingly, the Gospels clearly depict the women as being much braver and more loyal than the men. The apostles, the very ones whom Jesus had specially called and with whom he had spent the previous number of years teaching, encouraging and calling them to be witnesses to him, let him down in his hour of need and despaired when he was arrested. On Easter Sunday we find them locked up in a house, hiding and frightened.

The Two Disciples on the Road to Emmaus
One of these stories is about two disciples who were walking from Jerusalem to Emmaus – a small village about seven miles away – after the crucifixion (Luke 24:13–35).

> Now on that same day two of them were going to a village called Emmaus, about seven miles from Jerusalem, and talking with each other about all these things that had happened. While they were talking and discussing, Jesus

himself came near and went with them, but their eyes were kept from recognising him. And he said to them, 'What are you discussing with each other while you walk along?' They stood still, looking sad. Then one of them, whose name was Cleopas, answered him, 'Are you the only stranger in Jerusalem who does not know the things that have taken place there in these days?' He asked them, 'What things?' (Luke 24:3–19)

Read the whole text. What do you notice?

The disciples were filled with despair because they had hoped that Jesus would be their Saviour. They had seen him arrested, and although they had fled for fear of their lives, they had heard about his crucifixion, so they were terrified.

Then this stranger joins them on the road and asks what they are talking about. They are amazed at this question, and wonder what planet he has been living on, since the only thing most people in Jerusalem were talking about was the death of Jesus.

The stranger starts telling them how foolish they are, and how slow they are to believe. He starts talking to them about all the passages in Scripture that refer to the coming of the Messiah, the Saviour. The conversation is still going on when they reach Emmaus. So they ask him to come into the inn with them, because the sun was going down and it would be dangerous to travel at night.

He agrees. Later, in the inn, they sit down for a meal together. During the meal he takes the bread, blesses it and gives it to them. This was exactly what Jesus had done at the Last Supper. At that moment their eyes are opened, and they recognise him.

They then say something very important. They turn to each other and say, 'Wasn't it like a fire burning within us when he talked to us on the road and explained the Scriptures to us?'

So great is the impact of meeting Jesus that they immediately leave their meal, and despite the late hour, they rush back to Jerusalem. Their fear is gone. All they know is that something wonderful has happened to them, and they want to tell the whole world about it.

Christians believe that the resurrection marks the victory of Christ over death. It calls us to a living relationship with the Risen Christ in our lives and to a courageous witness to him.

The two disciples might have worried that Jesus would criticise them. After all, they abandoned him and allowed themselves to be overcome with fear. Instead, when Jesus appears to them, he does not judge their behaviour. He does not criticise or condemn them or mention their weakness. Instead he comforts and consoles them. All he refers to is their lack of faith: they should have believed the Scriptures and believed his words and promises.

All of those who experienced the Risen Christ had an extraordinary increase in their faith.

- Mary Magdalene moved from tears to exultation (John 20:11–18).
- The disciples on the road to Emmaus moved from confusion to clarity and from fear to joy (Luke 24:36–42).
- Doubting Thomas moved to belief (John 20: 24–29).
- The Disciples on the sea of Tiberias, especially Peter, moved from shame to faithfulness (John 21:1–19).

In all these meetings Jesus invites us to change our way of thinking, to accept that the love of God removes all fear and that he forgives all our sins. But do we believe this?

In appearing to the two disciples on the road to Emmaus we learn how much takes place during the walk, in their experience of the journey, of going to a different place, of walking with Jesus.

We too are all on a journey. We are all the time moving forward to our destination. Jesus is coming to meet us on our journey in order to accompany us and to walk alongside us like he did with the two disciples on the road to Emmaus. Can you experience the Risen Jesus walking with you as you make your journey?

Because of the Resurrection, all our Christian life should be under the standard of consolation and joy. This does not mean that we will always feel good, but it does mean that we will be friends with Jesus.

Reminder

Remember the awful despair of the two disciples fleeing Jerusalem after the terrible murder of Jesus and the total end of all their hopes.

Remember how he brought them deeper into their spiritual selves by asking them a series of questions.

And then remember the incredible joy they had when they recognised him, and how this changed them from terrified, fleeing people, to courageous, enthusiastic disciples of Christ.

Remember also from Reflection 3 about the prodigal son, how his life was utterly changed by going back to his father, and how he was welcomed as the honoured son.

Closing Prayer: The Our Father

Remember

- Keep reflecting on your purpose in life, and keep practising the daily Examen and daily prayer.
- Keep listening for God's question, 'What do you want?'
- Keep in mind that you are a loved sinner.
- Do you need to walk down a different street?
- What do you need healing from?
- Can you see that in your deepest self you are really like God, because that is the way that God made you?
- Jesus suffered and died out of love for you.
- Are you open to hearing what God is calling you to?
- Can you take inspiration from the example of Mary when you need courage and help?
- Can you keep begging for the grace of light to illuminate your darkness?
- Can you experience the Risen Jesus walking with you?

Reflection 12:

So, What Do YOU Want?

Read the following poem:

> I met her at a party. We loved it at the start.
> Within three weeks of meeting her, she kind of won my heart.
> I'd heard some things about her, some good things and some bad.
> I was told not to trust her: she was cunning, sly and smart.
> She made me feel so happy, so I pushed these things aside.
> But soon things started changing, problems rushed in like high tide.
> She made me borrow money, it didn't feel so nice.
> But when I couldn't borrow she made me steal and beg.
> And if I couldn't fund her she left me ill in bed.
> See, what I didn't think of when I took her in my arms.
> Was people tried to warn me that she would cause me harm.
> So if you ever meet her. I'll tell you who she is.
> Stay clear and do what I did and put her in the bin.
> She's really very famous, her name is Heroin.

'She' could also be called various other names: Cocaine, Cannabis, Vodka, Whiskey, Wine, Gambling, Sex, Power, Celebrity. You know who 'she' is for you.

This poem was written by a prisoner while still inside (From *Faith Inside,* Redemptorist Publications 2016, p. 98).

So, What Do YOU Want?
Where do you want to go with your life? That is the question that Jesus asked the first disciples, as we saw in Reflection 2. That same question, at the end of this journey – and indeed all through it – is addressed to you.

Can you now choose to turn your life back to God? Can you look for your own freedom? Can you turn the key of your prison door? It's on the inside of the door, and has been there all along.

Can you decide to use the following to help you on that journey?

(1) Daily Prayer

We should make prayer a central part of our day if we haven't done so already.

Start with a few minutes in the morning and the evening.

Ignatius found that like Jesus, spending time in prayer each day was very important. He said we should always talk to Jesus as one close friend would speak to another.

Remember, from Reflection 1, when the disciples asked Jesus to teach them how to pray, he said, 'whenever you pray, go into your room and shut the door and pray to your Father who is in secret, and your Father who sees in secret will reward you' (Matthew 6:6).

That room is deep inside each one of us where God is to be found and where God speaks to us.

Don't be afraid to express your real feelings, your anger, hurt, joys and sorrows.

It could be like the following: 'Jesus, sometimes I've been angry with you and felt you let me down. Help me to trust that you have a loving plan for me, a plan I find sometimes hard to understand, especially in the mess that I am in because of my addiction. Help me to trust you.'

Jesus then taught his disciples the Our Father. Pray it every day. (Go back to the Our Father in Reflection 5).

(2) Daily Review / Examen

- Each night before you go to bed spend a few moments reviewing your day in the presence of God.
- First give thanks for all that was good.
- Then look at all the people that you met during the day and the experiences you had, and note that Jesus has been present in all of them, as he has in you.

- Then look at what could have been better.
- Ask God to help you tomorrow.
  (See the Daily Review / Examen in Reflection 3 for help, and the Twelve Steps in Reflections 1 and 2)

(3) Read the Bible

Make time to read the Bible each day, just one psalm or one story from the Gospels through which you will learn much about the kind of person that Jesus was. Or look at the following day's readings at Mass, or the passages that will come up in your church's service on the following Sunday. For those who cannot read, audio versions are available, as are some helpful videos. Look at how Jesus lived his life and how he interacted with all those he met. He met and ate with people who were treated as outcasts in society and brought them peace. He did not join in their bad behaviour but he showed them a different way to live their lives that would bring them happiness.

He healed the sick, reached out to lepers with compassion, gave sight to the blind. In his day he met much human suffering and it affected him deeply.

Your suffering today also affects him deeply.

Jesus looks on everyone with deep compassion. When we become aware of his presence in our lives we can become aware of the peace and the healing of our body, mind and spirit.

(4) Go to Worship

Perhaps you could go to Mass or to service in your church on Sundays and so get a deeper awareness of how communal worship helps us to connect better with our Christian family. Listen to the readings and hear the message of Jesus. We need support sometimes. Our path need not be lonely.

(5) Look at Changes You Need to Make

Take time to reflect on the changes you need to make in your life. Again it is important to do this reflection within the context of your prayer.

The important questions for you are:

- Does your present behaviour have a reasonable chance of getting you what you want in life?
- Will your present behaviour take you in the direction you want to go?
- If you keep doing what you are doing, will you get what you want?
- Or will you end up stuck in a mess?
- Do you need to change the way you think?
- What is your body telling you about the road you are on in life?

Having outlined the changes you need to make in your life then pray about the following:

- It will be your choice whether to go to AA, or counselling, or a treatment programme.
- It will be your choice whether or not you to turn your life back to prayer which many in addiction have found helpful in the past.
- It will be your choice to hold on to the resentment, jealousy, anger and hurt, or whatever you blame for your addiction.
- It will be your choice to do nothing about your life and instead continue your self-abuse.

In the Spiritual Exercises, Ignatius asks us to be open to choosing what God wants. If you do this, you will be able to live with a new freedom.

(6) Check Your Direction

Check the direction that you are taking every day and make sure that you are on the road to your goals or destination. If you're on the roundabout or going down the slip road, get off it. Get back on to the road towards your destination, which is to live with God for ever. This may mean being open to seeking help. AA have a saying, 'I've got to change my way of thinking if I'm going to stay sober'.

(7) Spend Some Time Reflecting

A lot of people end up in prison because of alcohol and other drugs. Many others have escaped being caught but are still stuck in their own prison of addiction. So what do you do if you are faced with an addiction?

Well suppose your problem was cancer, what would you do? You would go to a doctor and get help. Likewise, with an addiction you need to get help. That might be AA, NA or an anger management course.

You have a choice here, get help and deal with your problem, or continue the same behaviour until you reach rock bottom.

God created us to live our lives to the full, to enjoy life and not to be going around half brain dead from alcohol and other drugs. But God gave us free will. He made us intelligent beings. We have a higher intelligence than animals. Your dog has limited intelligence. He follows other dogs. He doesn't have your mind and will and intelligence. Can you use the higher intelligence you've got in a better way?

You have a choice. Keep feeding your addiction or your anger, and keep getting into trouble, or choose the opposite. You have to stop and think.

Instead of thinking, 'I need a drug to fill my selfish need', STOP, see the red lights flashing in your brain and think of the consequences of your actions before you act. Think of the harm you will do to yourself and others if you give in.

Can you begin to think of other people instead of always thinking of yourself?

You will only do this through prayer and asking God to help you each time you are tempted. You pray this in the Our Father: lead us not into temptation but deliver us from evil. Keep praying this.

You have to avoid the drug dealers. Think of the drug dealers that use you. The big ones are not off their heads on drugs. No, they are only interested in getting your money to fund the high lifestyle they live. With your money they buy luxury villas in Spain and elsewhere, big cars, dine in expensive restaurants, and laugh all the way to the bank with your money, while your life is left in ruins. Stop supporting them. Learn to say NO, and walk away.

Most of them are not in prison. They are too smart for that, but they take full advantage of you and get you hooked. You have a choice: be strong, say no, and walk a different street. Read again the poem, 'My Autobiography in Five Chapters' in Reflection 4.

The prodigal son had to hit rock bottom before he turned back. When he did, God was waiting for him with outstretched arms. He is also waiting for you.

The journey to freedom from addiction is a long, slow and difficult one. Whatever setback you encounter, there is only one response needed: get up and start again. This is incredibly difficult as we blame ourselves for our failures and lose all hope of change, but remember the despair and hopelessness of the disciples and also the three falls of Jesus during the Way of the Cross, and how all these were transformed by the resurrection.

Some day you may be ready for the twelfth step of the Twelve-Step Programme:

> Having had a spiritual awakening as a result of the AA Steps, Examination and Promises, we try to carry this message to compulsive addicts of any kind, and to practice these principles in our affairs.

Read the following reflection:

Detachment ... with Love

> *Detachment* means separating the personality you love from the disease you despise.

> It means accepting the afflicted one unconditionally as an individual of worth and dignity, while steadfastly rejecting the destructive influences of alcoholism and/or drugs on yourself and on the family members in your care.

Detachment means caring enough to relinquish your fantasies and fictions to accept the full reality of the alcoholic condition and the reality of yourself as well.

Detachment means letting go of anger, resentment, fear, recrimination, self-justification, false pride, self-condemnation and self-pity, so that decisions can be made and actions taken dispassionately in loving wisdom and with calm resolve.

Detachment is a course of constructive independence, not a license for retaliatory self-indulgence. It is an assertion of your human rights, not a usurpation of those of the alcoholic. It is a tool for serenity, not a weapon for retribution.

Detachment means being
...objective, but not indifferent;
...flexible, but not indecisive;
...firm, but not hard;
...wise, but not clever;
...patient, but not resigned;
...strong, but not overbearing;
...resolute, but not stubborn;
...compassionate, but not indulgent.

Detachment is profound love, wrapped in understanding and bound by courage, helping you to live with serenity and fulfilment in spite of the environment, and in constant readiness for the alcoholic's decision for sobriety ... even without its expectation.

Anonymous

Closing Prayer
Jesus said to His disciples and therefore to each one of us:

'Do not let your hearts be troubled. Believe in God; believe also in me. In my Father's house there are many dwelling places. If it were not so, would I have told you that I go to prepare a place for you? And if I go and prepare a place for you, I will come again and will take you to myself, so that where I am, there you may be also. And you know the way to the place where I am going.' Thomas said to him, 'Lord, we do not know where you are going. How can we know the way?' Jesus said to him, 'I am the way and the truth and the life. No one comes to the Father except through me.'

Reminder

- Keep reflecting on 'my purpose in life' and keep practising the daily Examen and daily prayer.
- Keep listening for God's question, 'What do you want?'
- Keep in mind that you are a loved sinner.
- Do you need to walk down a different street?
- What do you need healing from?
- Can you see that in your deepest self you are really like God, because that is the way that God made you?
- Jesus suffered and died out of love for you.
- Are you open to hearing what God is calling you to?
- Can you take inspiration from the example of Mary when you need courage and help?
- Can you keep begging for the grace of light to illumine your darkness?
- Can you experience the Risen Jesus walking with you?
- So, what do YOU want?

Afterword by Peter McVerry SJ

Ignatius was a soldier who loved wine, women and song (though not necessarily in that order) and dreamt of finding fame and fortune through his exploits on the battlefield. However, a cannonball shattered not just his leg but his dream. While recuperating, Ignatius decided to change his life completely and devote himself to the service of God. The Spiritual Exercises are the fruit of this life-changing experience. They are therefore ideally suited to anyone who seeks to change their life but may not know where to start.

Martina Killeavy takes some elements of the Spiritual Exercises and the Twelve-Step Programme, and asks searching questions, which a person is encouraged to answer, as honestly as possible, in total confidence. It can be used in a wide variety of settings, not only with prisoners as part of their rehabilitation, but also by individuals, either on their own or with a spiritual guide, or with groups, such as in a parish setting, or pupils in a school. It provides a structured framework to facilitate change.

I have been visiting prisons on a regular basis for over forty years, trying to support prisoners in their desire to change, both during their imprisonment and on release. Sometimes a person will ask me, 'Are you not frightened going into the prisons?' I reply, 'No, never'. They have the impression that prisons are full of bad, dangerous people. Our prisons are full of people who have done bad things but are not bad people. Of course, some are people who have done very bad things, who have killed or raped or are high up in the drug distribution business. But over 70% of those in Irish prisons have an addiction, and most of them are in prison because of their addiction. They have robbed, shoplifted or sold drugs to pay for their own habit. The majority of them would love help to overcome their addiction, but often that help is not readily available. Others are homeless, others again have mental health problems, which have led them to repeatedly commit public order offences which are, in themselves, relatively minor. If suitably housed, or adequately treated in the community, many of them would not be in prison.

Some of those in prison have had horrific experiences, of child abuse, violence, or the loss of the only close relationship in their life. Many of them were themselves victims of crime before they made other people victims of crime. On one visit to a prison, I met with nine prisoners. Afterwards, I reflected on their lives – six of them were known to me to have been abused as children, the other three I did not know well enough to be able to say. Their inability to cope with those experiences led them to self-medicate, to erase the painful memories and feelings by using illegal drugs or alcohol. That addiction led them into crime to pay for their 'medication'.

In my experience, the majority of prisoners would love to change their lives, but the odds are stacked against them. Indeed, most of us find it hard to change, as we have developed fixed mind-sets and established patterns of behaviour. How much harder, then, is it for people who are released from prison, back into homelessness, or with their addiction or mental health issues untreated? They often feel powerless to change; change means letting go of what is familiar, losing control and facing a new, unknown reality, with few supports. But to acknowledge that feeling of powerlessness is to discover the need of a Higher Power to help them on the path of change, a key component of both the Spiritual Exercises and the AA / NA programmes.

Prisoners often have low self-esteem, often coming from areas of deprivation, with low levels of education, and little or no employment history. People are constantly putting them down. They expect very little, as that has been their life experience to date. To come to the belief that 'I am more than this' is the beginning of change. That means recognising that 'I am loveable' despite my offences. None of us are perfect, every saint had their dark side. No one, not even the worst offender, is a one-dimensional person; they are not defined by their crime, but it may be a struggle for them to separate their good side from their dark side.

Martina, like Ignatius in the Spiritual Exercises, starts by posing the question, 'What do YOU want?' Our first answers may be very superficial, but as we reflect more, we begin to get in touch with our deepest desires. We are called to make a choice. The courage to choose a different path rests on the belief that we are loved by God, unconditionally, to such an extent that God forgives us for everything we have done. While most of us know we are sinners, we have to come to realise that we are not only sinners, but sinners, forgiven and loved. Ignatius believed that since God gave us our imagination, we should use it! The story of the Prodigal Son, in Reflection Four, retold with great imagination, is a very powerful call to the realisation that we are forgiven and loved, despite what we may have done in our past. That realisation changes everything.

Prisoners are acutely conscious that they have sinned. When hearing confessions of prisoners, I hear the remorse in their voice. They are truly sorry for the hurt they have caused to others, including their family, who also often suffer the consequences of their offences or their addiction. I tell them that God has forgiven them, now the hard part is to forgive themselves. None of us can reach a place of wholeness unless we can forgive ourselves.

We are all in need of healing. Prisoners are aware of their need for healing, from past hurts, from being rejected, from low self-esteem, depression or addiction. Reflection Five calls us to reflect on this need for healing. The story of the paralytic, healed by Jesus, again told with great imagination, can convince us that there is nothing in our lives, or in our history, that cannot be healed.

Gratitude is at the heart of the Spiritual Exercises, and it begins with gratitude for being forgiven and loved. Gratitude then leads to trust, trust in a Higher Power, which the Spiritual Exercises identify as God. That gives us the confidence to love ourselves, despite our failings and low self-esteem. Until we can believe that we are loveable, we cannot believe that we are loved by God. Reflection Six leads us to the conviction that we are made in the image and likeness of God and therefore we are of infinite value to God. This realisation allows us to deal with the difficulties of life, to face confusion, doubts and difficult moments, to get up when we fall, and to let go of anger, resentments, and self-condemnation. It helps prisoners, indeed all of us, to move from being a victim of past experiences to becoming an agent of future change.

The Spiritual Exercises challenge us to confront our 'attachments', which prevent change, to free ourselves from them, and to discover a new freedom to live life differently. Change comes not from outside ourselves but from within, through self-awareness. The Spiritual Exercises, and the AA / NA programmes are about creating the conditions that allow us to identify the changes we need to make in our lives and give us the confidence and motivation to make them. Our imagination allows us to imagine who we can be, despite the addictions and negativity which afflict our lives.

The recognition that Jesus was arrested, jailed, convicted in a kangaroo-court, rejected by the religious and civil authorities, and sentenced to death on a cross helps prisoners to identify with him and to realise that despite their own arrest, conviction, going to jail and being rejected by many, they still possess a goodness and value that is unique to them, even if others do not see this.

Many prisoners, when they reach the point of changing their lives, want to help others. They recognise the importance of the help they themselves have received from others. They want to give something back to others who are in prison or addicted. Some prisoners volunteer to act as 'listeners' while serving their sentence, that is, they are available to listen to and support other prisoners who are feeling low, depressed or perhaps suicidal. Others learn first-aid while in prison so that they can assist someone while waiting for the medical staff to arrive. On release, they often want to get involved in organisations that work with drug users or ex-prisoners. Our self-esteem depends on our belief that we have something to give to others. Prisoners understand that the unique gift which they have to give is their own experience of crime or addiction, and many want to help others avoid the pitfalls that they fell into.

Finally, the belief that there is something beyond this life, with all its problems and difficulties, and that we will be given a place with a God who loves us, despite our sinfulness, gives hope where hope may be in short supply.

In short, this book leads people through a process that enables change. It is a powerful tool which can transform peoples' lives and deserves to be widely distributed.

Peter McVerry SJ is founder of the Peter McVerry Trust

Summary of Reflections

Reflection 1: St Ignatius and the Spiritual Exercises
Great sinners often became great Saints. Such was the story of Ignatius.

He asked himself a question that most of us ask, 'Why was I born?'

He gave us 3 great techniques to find freedom in our lives.

- Reflecting on what my purpose in life is.
- Getting into the habit of doing a daily Examen of my thoughts, emotions and actions, and asking myself do I find God in all things and situations?
- Making time each day for prayer.

In other words, he invites us to turn our lives back to God.

The first three steps of the Twelve-Step Programme have a similar message:

- I accept that I need to change my life and turn myself over to a Higher Power.
- I come to believe that a Power greater than myself could restore me to sanity.
- I make a decision to turn my will and my life over to the care of God *as I understand him.*

Reflection 2: Your Image of God
This reflection looks at your image of God. Take time to reflect on your image of God.

There is a brief outline of the life of Jesus.

How it all began: a reflection on John 1:35–39 taking the question Jesus asked Andrew and his companion who set out to follow him: 'What do you want'?

Hear God ask you that same question and consider how you might respond.

In doing this continue to look at steps 4–11 of the Twelve-Step Programme.

Reflection 3: The Negative Forces of Sin in the World

We continue to look at the negative force of sin in the world in the story of the Prodigal Son. The son left home seeking freedom. Unfortunately, he sought this in all the wrong areas: addictions and bad relationships. In the end, when he had lost everything, he came to his senses. He then started his journey back to God.

How did he find freedom from his addictions?

In looking at your own journey home it is also helpful to look at the daily Examen or review.

Reflection 4: Despite My Sinfulness, I Am Loved by God

Here we look at what the Prodigal Son discovered when he decided to turn his life back to God. Despite his sins and weakness, he discovered that he is loved by God who is full of mercy. He also discovered that this loving Father gives us freedom to make our own choices. He is now free to choose which road he wants to follow.

So are you – what road do you wish to follow?

Reflection 5: God's Mercy and Healing

We then look at the healing power of our loving God.

We take the story of the Paralytic in Luke 5:17–26.

We focus on the power of friendship, or for you it may be the influence and power of your AA group, or counselling or residential centre.

We then ask are you more frightened by your own goodness than by your own darkness?

Our own darkness may be more familiar to us, and therefore easier to live with than with the threat of changing.

Reflection 6: Love of God and Love of Self

Having discovered how much God loves us we ask the question, 'Do I love myself?' How would you describe your own self-image or self-esteem? What may have caused your low self-image or low self-esteem? Can you begin to believe in yourself and make different choices for your future? Can you begin to see that you are a unique child of God?

Reflection 7: The Passion and Death of Jesus

If we ever doubted how much God loves us we should look at the Passion and Death of Jesus. This shows us in graphic terms how much he loves us and how we are forgiven. He was crucified on a cross for us, although he was innocent, and two criminals who were not innocent hung on either side of him.

One of them asked him for forgiveness.

Reflection 8: The Call of the King

When we were baptised we became children of God's family and received 'the call' to God's kingdom. We now are members of two families: the family we were born into and a much bigger family which is God's family, the Church.

How have we responded to this call? Are you aware of being a member of God's family? Do you have gifts and talents that you can use to build up God's kingdom? Are you using these?

Here we see what our ultimate calling in life is and what we mean by freedom to choose.

Reflection 9: Saying 'Yes' to God: The Response of Mary

Saying 'yes' to God is sometimes not easy, especially if I have never thought of it before now.

One example of saying 'yes' to God and the underlying fear that may attach to it is that of Our Lady. She said 'yes' to God without fully understanding the implications of her yes. She did this as a great act of faith.

Can I make an act of faith by turning my life around without fully seeing the outcome at this moment, but trusting in God as Our Lady did?

Reflection 10: Temptations

Despite our best intentions to turn back our lives to God we are confronted with temptations.

Nobody is free of them.

We look at how Jesus himself was tempted by the evil one and how he came through the struggle through prayer and his constant trust in God his Father.

Nobody said it would be easy, but those who learn to resist the temptations to alcohol or other drugs, or other addictions are grateful to the higher force in their lives for being able to do so.

A good time to reflect on the Promises of AA is when we choose sobriety.

Reflection 11: The Resurrection of Jesus Christ

Every time we resist temptation we will begin to feel better about ourselves. Often we are tempted to ask ourselves, 'What's the point?'. Don't listen to that voice.

Just as Jesus came through death to new life, so you too can have your resurrection from the pain and darkness that addiction has brought into your life.

Reflection 12: So, What Do YOU Want?

Suggestions to move forward and daily supports to help you on the road to freedom.

Appendix Two

The Way of the Cross: A Prison Perspective, Led by Pope Francis, Good Friday 2020

The following meditations on the Stations of the Cross were prepared by the chaplaincy of the 'Due Palazzi', the House of Detention in Padua. Fourteen people were invited by Pope Francis to meditate on the Passion of our Lord Jesus Christ, bringing it to bear on their own situations. Those invited included five prisoners, a family that was the victim of a murder, the daughter of a man given a life sentence, a prison teacher, a civil magistrate, the mother of a prisoner, a catechist, a volunteer religious brother, a prison guard and a priest who was accused and then finally acquitted after eight years in the justice system.

They can be applied to the prisons we create for ourselves until we move towards freedom. They show the impact of addiction, not only on those who suffer directly from it, but also on their wider family, friends, and those who support them.

The stations can be viewed online at: https://www.youtube.com /watch?v=t4ExBAg992A.

First Station: Jesus is condemned to death.
(Meditation by a prisoner serving a life sentence)
Pilate addressed them once more, desiring to release Jesus; but they shouted out, 'Crucify, crucify him!' A third time he said to them, 'Why, what evil has he done? I have found in him no crime deserving death; I will therefore chastise him and release him.' But they were urgent, demanding with loud cries that he should be crucified. And their voices prevailed. So Pilate gave sentence that their demand should be granted. He released the man who had been thrown into prison for insurrection

and murder, whom they asked for; but Jesus he delivered up to their will (Lk 23:20–25).

Many times that cry, 'Crucify him, crucify him!' is shouted out in court-rooms and in newspapers. It is a cry I even heard against me: I was condemned, together with my father, to a life sentence. My crucifixion began when I was a child: when I think back I see myself curled up on the bus that took me to school, side-lined because of my stutter, with no friends. I started to work when I was small, without having a chance to study: ignorance prevailed over innocence. Then bullying stole what was left of childhood from this boy born in Calabria during the 1970s. I am more like Barabbas than Christ, yet the harshest condemnation remains that of my own conscience: at night I open my eyes and I desperately search for a light that will shine upon my story.

Alone in my cell, when I re-read the pages of the Passion of Christ, I burst into tears: after 29 years in prison I have not yet lost the capacity to cry, to feel ashamed of my past history and of the evil I did. I feel like Barabbas, Peter and Judas in one single person. I am repelled by my past, even though I know it is my story. I have lived for years under the restrictive conditions of Article 41b of the Prison Administration Act and my father died under the same conditions. Many times at night I heard him crying in his cell. He tried to hide it, but I knew. We were both plunged into deep darkness. In that non-life, however, I was always searching for something that would be life: strange to say, prison was my salvation. If, for some, I am still Barabbas, that does not make me angry: I know in my heart that the Innocent One, condemned like me, came to find me in prison to teach me about life.

Lord Jesus, despite the uproar, we glimpse you among the crowds shouting for you to be crucified; perhaps we too are among them, blind to the evil of which we are capable. From our cells we want to pray to your Father for all those who, like you, are condemned to death and for all those who would substitute their own for your supreme judgment.

Let us pray.

O God, lover of life, in the sacrament of Reconciliation, you always give us a new opportunity to experience your infinite mercy. We ask you to grant us the gift of wisdom so that we can see every man and woman as a temple of your Spirit and respect their inviolable dignity. Through Christ our Lord. Amen.

Second Station: Jesus takes up his Cross
(Meditation by two parents whose daughter was murdered)

The soldiers led him away inside the palace (that is, the Praetorium); and they called together the whole battalion. And they clothed him in a purple cloak, and plaiting a crown of thorns they put it on him. And they began to salute him, 'Hail, King of the Jews!' And they struck his head with a reed, and spat upon him, and they knelt down in homage to him. And when they had mocked him, they stripped him of the purple cloak, and put his own clothes on him. And they led him out to crucify him (Mk 15:16–20).

During that horrible summer our life as parents died together with that of our two daughters. One of them was murdered along with her closest friend by the blind violence of a ruthless man; the other, who miraculously survived, was forever deprived of her smile. Ours was a life of sacrifices based on work and family. We taught our children to respect others and to value serving the poor. We often ask ourselves: 'Why did it happen to us, this evil which engulfed us?'. We find no peace. Nor is justice, in which we had always trusted, able to relieve these deep wounds: our condemnation to suffering will never end.

Time has not eased the weight of the cross placed upon our shoulders: we are unable to forget our daughter who is no longer with us. We are elderly, more and more vulnerable and victims of the worst pain that can exist: surviving the death of a daughter.

This is difficult to say, but at the moment in which despair seems to take over, the Lord in different ways comes to meet us, giving us the grace to love one another as spouses, and to support one another, hard as it is. He invites us to keep the door of our home open to the poor and the despairing, welcoming whoever knocks, even if only for a bowl of soup. The commandment to perform acts of charity is for us a kind of salvation: we do not want to surrender to evil. God's love is truly capable of renewing life because, before us, his Son Jesus underwent human suffering so as to experience true compassion.

Lord Jesus, it pains us to see you struck, mocked and stripped, an innocent victim of inhumane cruelty. On this night of sorrow, we plead with your Father and entrust to him all those who have endured violence and evil.

Let us pray

O God, our justice and our redemption, who gave us your only Son and glorified him on the throne of the cross, instil your hope in our hearts so that we can recognize you present in the dark moments of our life. Comfort us in every affliction and support us in our trials as we await the coming of your kingdom. Through Christ our Lord. Amen.

Third Station: Jesus falls for the first time
(Meditation by a prisoner)

Surely he has borne our griefs and carried our sorrows; yet we esteemed him stricken, struck down by God, and afflicted. But he was wounded for our transgressions, he was bruised for our iniquities; upon him was the chastisement that made us whole, and with his stripes we are healed. All we like sheep have gone astray; we have turned every one to his own way; and the Lord has laid on him the iniquity of us all (Is 53:4–6).

It was the first time that I fell, but for me that fall was death: I took someone's life. It only takes a day to pass from a blameless life to committing an act which encompasses the violation of all the commandments. I feel like a modern version of that thief who implored Christ with the words 'Remember me!'. I imagine him less a penitent than someone conscious of being on the wrong path.

From my childhood I remember the cold and hostile environment in which I grew up. All it took was for me to figure out someone's weakness in order to transform it into a kind of entertainment. I was looking for real friends, I wanted to be accepted for who I was, but I was unable. I resented the happiness of others, I felt hamstrung, they asked of me only sacrifices and to obey the rules: I felt like a stranger to everyone and I sought revenge at all costs.

I hadn't realized that evil was slowly growing inside me. Until, one evening, my own hour of darkness struck: in a second, like an avalanche, the memories of all the injustices I had suffered in life exploded. Anger killed my kindness, I committed an evil immensely greater than any of those that I had received. Then, in prison the ill-treatment by others led me to self-hatred: I was close to ending it all, I had reached the limit. I had also ruined my family: because of me they lost their name and respectability; they had become merely the family of a murderer. I make no excuses and seek no reductions, I will serve my sentence to the end because in prison I have found people who have given me back the faith I had lost.

My first fall was failing to realize that goodness exists in this world. My second, the murder, was really its consequence, for I was already dead inside.

Lord Jesus, you, too, fell to the ground. Perhaps your first fall was the hardest because it was entirely new: the impact was hard and left you shaken. We entrust to your Father all those who are so caught up in themselves that they are unable to acknowledge the sins they have committed.

Let us pray.

O God, you raised mankind up when we had fallen. We ask you to come to help us in our weakness and to grant us eyes to see the signs of your love everywhere in our daily lives. Through Christ our Lord. Amen.

Fourth Station: Jesus meets his Mother
(Meditation by the mother of a prisoner)

Standing by the cross of Jesus were his mother, and his mother's sister, Mary the wife of Cleopas, and Mary Magdalene. When Jesus saw his mother, and the disciple whom he loved standing near, he said to his mother, 'Woman, behold, your son!' Then he said to the disciple, 'Behold, your mother!' And from that hour the disciple took her to his own home (Jn 19:25–27).

Not for a moment was I tempted to abandon my son in the face of his sentence. The day he was arrested changed our entire life: the whole family went into prison with him. Today people's judgment remains implacable: like a sharp knife, fingers pointed are against all of us, increasing the suffering we already bear in our hearts.

The wounds grow with each passing day; they take our breath away.

I feel Mother Mary close to me: she helps me not to give into despair and to cope with the pain. I've entrusted my son to her: only to Mary can I confide my fears, since she herself experienced them on the way to Calvary. In her heart she knew that her Son would not escape human evil, yet she did not abandon him. She stood there sharing in his suffering, keeping him company by her presence. I think of Jesus looking up, seeing those eyes so full of love, and not feeling alone.

I would like to do the same.

I blamed myself for my son's sins. I asked forgiveness also for my own responsibility. I beg for the mercy that only a mother is able to experience, so that my son can return to life after having paid for his crime. I pray constantly for him, so that day by day he can grow into a different man, capable once more of loving himself and others.

Lord Jesus, meeting your mother on the way of the cross is perhaps the most moving and most sorrowful of all.

Between your eyes and hers, we place all families and friends who feel pained and helpless before the fate of their loved ones.

Let us pray.

O Mary, Mother of God and Mother of the Church, faithful disciple of your Son, we turn to you and entrust to your loving gaze and to the care of your maternal heart the cry of all humanity which awaits with anguish the day when every tear will be wiped away from their faces. Amen.

Fifth Station: Simon of Cyrene helps Jesus carry the Cross (Meditation by a prisoner)
As they led him away, they seized one Simon of Cyrene, who was coming in from the country, and laid on him the cross, to carry it behind Jesus (Lk 23:26).

With my job I helped generations of children to believe in themselves. Then one day I found myself lying on the ground. It was as if they broke my back: my job was the pretext for a shameful conviction. I entered prison: prison entered my home. Since then I have become an outcast in the city: I have lost my name, I am now known by the crime of which I have been charged, I am no longer the master of my life. When I think about it, that child with worn-out shoes, wet feet, second-hand clothes comes to mind: that child was me, I was once that child. Then, one day, my arrest: three men in uniform, a rigid protocol, the prison that swallowed me alive in its concrete maw.

The cross they placed on my shoulders is a heavy one. Over time I have learned to live with it, to look it in the face, to call it by name: we spend many nights keeping each other company. Inside prisons, Simon of Cyrene is known by everyone: it is the second name of volunteers, of those who mount this Calvary to help carry a cross; they are people who reject the law of the pack and listen to their conscience. Simon of Cyrene, too, is my cellmate: I met him my first night in prison. He was a man who had lived on a bench for years, without affection or income. His only wealth was a box of candies. He has a sweet tooth, but he insisted that I bring it to my wife the first time she visited me: she burst into tears at that unexpected and thoughtful gesture.

I'm growing old in prison: I dream that one day, I will be able to trust others.

To become a Cyrenean, bringing joy to someone.

Lord Jesus, from the moment of your birth to the time you met a stranger who helped you carry your cross, you wanted to depend on our help. We too, like the Cyrene, desire to be close to our brothers and sisters and to help in offering the Father's mercy that breaks the yoke that oppresses them.

Let us pray.

O God, defender of the poor and comforter of the afflicted, strengthen us with your presence and help us to bear each day the easy yoke of your commandment of love. Through Christ our Lord. Amen.

Sixth Station: Veronica wipes the face of Jesus
(Meditation by a catechist)

My heart says to you, 'Your face, Lord, do I seek'. Hide not your face from me. Turn not your servant away in anger, you who have been my help. Cast me not off, forsake me not, O God of my salvation! (Ps 27: 8–9).

As a catechist, I wipe away many tears, letting them flow: they flood uncontrollably from hearts that are broken. Many times I meet despairing souls who, in the darkness of prison, try to find a reason for the evil that to them seems infinite. Their tears are those of defeat and loneliness, of remorse and lack of understanding. I often imagine Jesus here in prison in my stead: how would he wipe away the tears? How would he ease the anguish of these men who feel trapped by what they have become in yielding to evil?

Coming up with an answer is hard, often impossible within the limits of our petty human logic. The way pointed out to me by Christ is to contemplate, without fear, those faces marred by suffering. I am asked to remain there with them, respecting their silence, listening to their pain, and seeking to look beyond prejudice. In the same way that Christ looks at our own weaknesses and limitations with eyes full of love. Everyone, including those in prison, has an opportunity each day to become a new person, thanks to Christ's look which does not judge, but gives life and hope.

In this way, the tears that fall can become the seed of a beauty that was difficult even to imagine.

Lord Jesus, Veronica had pity on you: she encountered a suffering person and discovered the face of God. In prayer we entrust to your Father the men and women of our times who seek to wipe away the tears of so many of our brothers and sisters.

Let us pray.

O God, true light and source of all light, in weakness you reveal the power and radicalism of love. Imprint your face in our hearts, so that we can recognize you in all human suffering. Through Christ our Lord. Amen.

Seventh Station: Jesus falls for the second time
(Meditation by a prisoner)

Jesus said, 'Father, forgive them; for they know not what they do'. And they cast lots to divide his garments (Lk 23:34).

In the past, whenever I walked past a prison, I looked the other way: 'I will never end up in there', I said to myself. The times I did look, I felt sadness and darkness: I felt like I was walking past a cemetery of the living dead. Then one day, I ended up behind bars, together with my brother. As if that wasn't enough, I also brought my father and mother in there. From the foreign country it had been, the prison is now our home: we men were in one cell, our mother in another. I looked at them and I felt ashamed of myself. I no longer feel like I am a man. They are growing old in prison because of me.

I fell twice. The first time was when evil attracted me and I gave in: peddling drugs, in my eyes, was worth more than the work of my father, who was breaking his back ten hours a day. The second was when, after ruining the family, I began to ask myself: 'Who am I that Christ should die for me?'. The cry of Jesus – *'Father, forgive them; for they know not what they do'* – I saw reflected in my mother's eyes: she took on the shame of all the men of the house to save the family. And I saw it in the face of my father, as he secretly despaired in his cell. Only today can I admit it: in those years I didn't know what I was doing. Now that I know, I am trying to rebuild my life with the help of God. I owe it to my parents: years ago, they sold all that we had of value because they didn't want me to live on the street. I owe it above all to myself: the idea that evil can continue to guide my life is intolerable. This is what has become my way of the cross.

Lord Jesus, once again you have fallen to the ground: crushed by my attachment to evil, by my fear of not being able to become a better person. In faith we turn to your Father and pray for all those not yet able to break free from the power of Satan, from all his allurements and his manifold seductions.

Let us pray.

O God, you do not leave us in the darkness and shadow of death. Strengthen us in our weakness, free us from the bonds of evil and shield us by your power, so that we may forever sing of your mercy. Through Christ our Lord. Amen.

Eighth Station: Jesus meets the women of Jerusalem (Meditation by the daughter of a man sentenced to life imprisonment)

There followed him a great multitude of the people, and of women who bewailed and lamented him. But Jesus turning to them said, 'Daughters of Jerusalem, do not weep for me, but weep for yourselves and for your children. For behold, the days are coming when they will say, 'Blessed are the barren, and the wombs that never bore, and the breasts that never nursed!' Then they will begin to say to the mountains, 'Fall on us'; and to the hills, 'Cover us' (Lk 23:27–30).

How many times, as the daughter of someone in prison, have I been asked: 'You love your father: do you ever think about the pain he inflicted on his victims?'. Over these years I have never failed to answer: 'Of course, it is impossible for me not to think about it'. But then I ask them this question: 'Have you ever thought that, of all the victims of my father's action, I was the first? For twenty-eight years I have been serving the sentence of growing up without a father'. For all these years I have lived with anger, restlessness, sadness: his absence is a heavy burden to bear. I have travelled throughout Italy, from south to north, to stay with him: I know its cities not for their monuments but for the prisons I have visited. I seem to be like Telemachus when he went in search of his father Odysseus: my journey takes me to Italian prisons and loved ones.

Years ago, I missed love because I am the daughter of a prisoner, my mother fell prey to depression, the family collapsed. I was left, with my small salary, to bear the weight of this sorry story. Life forced me to become an adult without ever being a child. In my home, everything is a *via crucis*: Dad is one of those sentenced to life imprisonment. The day I got married, I dreamed of having him beside me: even then he was thinking of me, though hundreds of kilometres away. 'Such is life!', I say, to encourage myself. It's true: there are parents who, out of love, learn to wait for their children to grow up. In my own case, for love, I wait for my Dad's return. For people like us, hope is a duty.

Lord Jesus, we see your words to the women of Jerusalem as a warning to each of us. Those words invite us to conversion, to pass from a sentimental religiosity to a faith rooted in your word. We pray for those who are forced to bear the burden of shame, the suffering of abandonment, the lack of a presence. And for each of us, that the sins of parents may not fall on their children.

Let us pray.

O God, Father of all kindness, you do not abandon your children in the trials of life. Give us the grace to be able to rest in your love and to enjoy forever the consolation of your presence. Through Christ our Lord. Amen.

Ninth Station: Jesus falls for the third time
(Meditation by a prisoner)

It is good for a man that he bear the yoke in his youth. Let him sit alone in silence when he has laid it on him; let him put his mouth in the dust — there may yet be hope; let him give his cheek to the one who strikes him, and be filled with insults. For the Lord will not cast off forever, but, though he cause grief, he will have compassion according to the abundance of his steadfast love (Lamentations 3:27–32).

Falling down is never pleasant; but beyond the fact that it is unpleasant, falling over and over again becomes itself a kind of condemnation, as if one is no longer capable of remaining standing. As a man, I have fallen all too many times: I have also gotten up many times. In prison I often think about how many times a child falls to the ground before learning to walk: I am coming to think that these are preparations for all the times when we will fall as adults. As a child, my home was like a prison: I lived in fear of punishment, alternating between the melancholy of adults and the carefreeness of children. Of those years I remember Sister Gabriella, the only happy image: she was the only one who saw the best in me. Like Peter, I have sought and found many excuses for my mistakes: the strange fact is that a fragment of goodness always remained alive in me.

I became a grandfather in prison: I didn't experience my daughter's pregnancy. One day, I will tell my granddaughter the story of only the goodness I have found and not the evil I have done. I will tell her about the one who, when I lay fallen on the ground, brought me the mercy of God. In prison, the worst form of despair is to think that life no longer has meaning. It is the greatest suffering: of all the lonely people in the world, you feel like the loneliest. It is true that my life was shattered into a thousand pieces, but the wonderful thing is that those pieces can still be put together. It is not easy, but it is the only thing that still makes sense here.

Lord Jesus, you fall a third time to the ground and, when everyone thinks that this is the end, once again you get up. We confidently put ourselves in the hands of your Father and entrust to him all those who feel imprisoned in the abyss of their errors, so that they may be granted the strength to get up and the courage to let themselves be helped.

Let us pray.

O God, strength of those who hope in you, you give peace to those who follow your teachings. Sustain our staggering steps, raise us when we fall through our unfaithfulness. Pour the balm of consolation and the wine of hope on our wounds. Through Christ our Lord. Amen.

Tenth Station: Jesus is stripped of his garments (Meditation by a prison teacher)
When the soldiers had crucified Jesus they took his garments and made four parts, one for each soldier; also his tunic. But the tunic was without seam, woven from top to bottom; so they said to one another, 'Let us not tear it, but cast lots for it to see whose it shall be.' This was to fulfil the Scripture, 'They parted my garments among them, and for my clothing they cast lots' (Jn 19:23–24).

As a teacher in a prison, I see people entering jail deprived of everything: stripped of all dignity because of the crimes they have committed, stripped of all respect for themselves and for others. Every day I see how they become more and more dependent behind bars: they need me even to help write a letter. These are the unsettled lives entrusted to my care: helpless, frustrated by their weakness, frequently deprived of even the ability to understand the wrong they have done. At times, however, they are like newborn babies who can still be formed. I sense that their lives can start over in another direction, definitively turning away from evil.

My strength, however, is fading day by day. Encountering daily all this anger, pain and hidden malice ends up wearing down even the most experienced of us. I chose this work after my mother was killed in a head-on collision by a young drug addict: I decided to respond immediately to that evil with good. But even though I love this job, I sometimes struggle to find the strength to carry on.

In so sensitive a service, we need to feel that we are not abandoned, in order to be able to support the many lives entrusted to us, lives that each day run the risk of ruin.

Lord Jesus, when we gaze at you stripped of your garments we feel embarrassed and ashamed. Beginning with the first man, in the face of the naked truth we started to run away. We hide behind masks of respectability and clothe ourselves with lies, frequently with the threadbare rags of the poor, exploited by our greedy thirst for money and power. May the Father have mercy on us and patiently help us to become more simple, more transparent, more authentic: ready to abandon definitively the weapons of hypocrisy.

Let us pray.

O God, you set us free by your truth. Strip us of our interior resistance and clothe us with your light, that we may be the reflection of your glory in the world. Through Christ our Lord. Amen.

The Eleventh Station: Jesus is nailed to the Cross
(Meditation by a priest accused and later acquitted)

When they came to the place which is called The Skull, there they crucified him, and the criminals, one on the right and one on the left. And Jesus said, 'Father, forgive them; for they know not what they do'. And they cast lots to divide his garments. And the people stood by, watching; but the rulers scoffed at him, saying, 'He saved others; let him save himself, if he is the Christ of God, his Chosen One!' The soldiers also mocked him, coming up and offering him vinegar, and saying, 'If you are the King of the Jews, save yourself!' There was also an inscription over him, 'This is the King of the Jews'. One of the criminals who were hanged railed at him, saying, 'Are you not the Christ? Save yourself and us!' But the other rebuked him, saying, 'Do you not fear God, since you are under the same sentence of condemnation? And we indeed justly; for we are receiving the due reward of our deeds; but this man has done nothing wrong'. And he said, 'Jesus, remember me when you come in your kingly power'. And he said to him, 'Truly, I say to you, today you will be with me in Paradise' (Luke 23:33–43).

Christ nailed to the Cross. How often, as a priest, have I meditated on this page of the Gospel. When later, one day, they put me on a cross, I felt the full weight of that wood: the accusation was made in words as hard as nails, the ascent became steep, suffering weighed me down. The darkest moment was seeing my name pasted outside the courtroom: at that moment I realized that I was a guiltless man forced to prove his innocence. I hung on the cross for ten years: my Way of the Cross was populated with dossiers, suspicions, accusations, insults. Each time I was in the courtroom, I looked for the crucifix: I kept my eyes fixed on it as the law investigated my story.

For a moment, shame led me to think that it would be better to end it all. But then I decided to remain the priest I always was. I never thought of lessening my cross, even when the law permitted it. I chose to submit myself to a regular trial: I owed it to myself, to the young men I taught during the years at the seminary, to their families. While I was climbing my Calvary, I found them all along the way: they became my Cyreneans, they bore the weight of the cross with me, they dried my many tears. Together with me, many of them prayed for the young man who accused me: they never stopped. The day on which I was fully acquitted, I found myself happier than I had been ten years before: I experienced first-hand God working in my life. Hanging on the cross, I discovered the meaning of my priesthood.

Lord Jesus, the love you showed us to the end led you to the cross. Dying, you still forgive us and give us life. We entrust to your Father all those innocent men and women who throughout history have suffered unjust condemnation. May your words resound in their hearts: 'Today you will be with me in Paradise'.

Let us pray.

God, source of mercy and forgiveness, who reveal yourself in the sufferings of humanity, enlighten us with the grace that flows from the wounds of the Crucified One and grant us perseverance in faith throughout the dark night of trial. Through Christ our Lord. Amen.

The Twelfth Station: Jesus dies on the Cross
(Meditation by a civil magistrate)

It was now about the sixth hour, and there was darkness over the whole land until the ninth hour, while the sun's light failed; and the curtain of the temple was torn in two. Then Jesus, crying with a loud voice, said, 'Father, into your hands I commit my spirit'. And having said this he breathed his last (Luke 23:44–46).

As a civil magistrate, I cannot crucify a man, any man, to the sentence he is serving: that would mean sentencing him a second time. He has to pay for the wrong he did: not to do so would mean trivializing his crimes, justifying the intolerable actions he carried out that caused physical and moral suffering to others.

True justice, however, is possible only through a mercy that does not crucify an individual for ever, but becomes a guide in helping him to get up and to realize the goodness that, for all the wrong he has done, is never completely extinguished in his heart. Only by finding his own humanity again will the convicted person be able to see himself in others, in the victim to whom he caused such pain. As much as his path of rebirth can be tortuous and the risk of falling back into evil remains always present, there is no other way to try to rebuild his own personal and communal history.

The severity of a sentence puts a person's hope to a hard test: it helps him to reflect and question whether the reasons for his actions might become an opportunity to consider himself from another perspective. To do this, though, he has to learn how to recognize the person hidden behind the crime committed. In this process, it sometimes becomes possible to glimpse a horizon that can instil hope in that person and once his sentence has been served, to return to society and hope that people will welcome him back after having rejected him.

For all of us, even those convicted of a crime, are children of the same human family.

Lord Jesus, you died as the result of a corrupt conviction, handed down by unjust judges terrified by the irrepressible force of the Truth. We entrust to your Father all magistrates, judges and lawyers and ask that they may be upright in carrying out their service to the State and its citizens, especially those who suffer the effects of poverty.

Let us pray.

O God, King of justice and peace, you heard in the cry of your Son the cry of all humanity. Teach us not to identify the person with the wrong he has done and help us to see in everyone the living flame of your Spirit. Through Christ our Lord. Amen.

The Thirteenth Station: Jesus is taken down from the Cross (Meditation by a volunteer religious Brother)

Now there was a man named Joseph from the Jewish town of Arimathea. He was a member of the council, a good and righteous man, who had not consented to their purpose and deed, and he was looking for the kingdom of God. This man went to Pilate and asked for the body of Jesus. Then he took it down and wrapped it in a linen shroud, and laid him in a rock-hewn tomb where no one had ever yet been laid (Lk 23:50–53).

Prisoners have always been my teachers. Sixty years ago, I went into prisons as a volunteer friar and I have always blessed the day when, for the first time, I encountered this hidden world. Seeing their faces, I came to realize with clarity that I could have been in their place, had my life taken a different direction. We Christians frequently fall into the illusion of feeling that we are better than others, as our care for the poor allows us to stand as judges of others, condemning them as many times as we want, without any appeal.

In his life, Christ willingly chose to take his stand with the least: he travelled the forgotten peripheries of the world in the midst of thieves, lepers, prostitutes, scoundrels. He wanted to share the experience of poverty, solitude, anxiety. I have always thought that that was the real meaning of his words: 'I was in prison and you came to visit me' (Mt 25:36).

Passing by one cell after another, I see the death that lives within. Prison continues to bury individuals alive: theirs are stories that no one wants to hear any longer. Each time, Christ says to me again: 'Keep going, don't stop. Take them in your arms again'. I cannot help but listen to him: even within the worst of persons, he is always there, however obscured is their memory of him. I just need to halt my hectic pace, stop in silence before those faces marred by evil and listen to them with mercy. This is the only way I know to accept that person, and avert my gaze from the mistake he made. Only in this way will he be able to trust and regain the strength to surrender to God's goodness, and see himself differently.

Lord Jesus, your body, disfigured by such great evil, is now wrapped in a shroud and consigned to the bare earth: here is the new creation. To your Father, we entrust the Church, born from your pierced side, that she may never give up in the face of failure and appearances, but persevere in bringing to all the joyful message of our salvation.

Let us pray.

O God, beginning and end of all things, in the Passover of Christ you redeemed all humanity. Grant us the wisdom of the Cross that we may abandon ourselves to your will with a spirit of joy and gratitude. Through Christ our Lord. Amen.

The Fourteenth Station: Jesus is laid in the tomb
(Meditation by a corrections officer)
It was the day of Preparation, and the Sabbath was beginning. The women who had come with him from Galilee followed, and saw the tomb, and

how his body was laid; then they returned, and prepared spices and ointments. On the Sabbath they rested according to the commandment (Lk 23:54–56).

In my mission as a corrections officer, every day I experience first-hand the suffering of those who live in prison. It is not easy to be faced with someone who yielded to evil and inflicted immense harm on others and their lives. In prison, an attitude of indifference can create even further harm in the history of someone who has failed and is paying his debt to justice. A colleague, who was my mentor, frequently repeated: 'Prison changes you: a good person can become a sadistic one. An evil person can become better'. The result also depends on me and a firm resolution is essential for achieving the goal of our work: that of offering another possibility to someone who did wrong. To attempt this, I cannot limit myself to opening and closing a cell, without doing this with a touch of humanity.

By respecting each person's tempo, human relations can once more flourish little by little within this oppressive world. It happens through gestures, attitudes and words that can make a difference, even if spoken in a low voice. I am not ashamed to exercise the permanent diaconate in wearing the uniform of which I am proud. I know suffering and despair: I experienced them as a child. My small wish is to be a point of reference for those I encounter behind bars. I work hard to keep hope alive in people left to themselves, frightened at the thought of one day leaving and possibly being rejected yet again by society.

In prison, I remind them that, with God, no sin will ever have the last word.

Lord Jesus, once more you are in the hands of men, but this time, they are the loving hands of Joseph of Arimathea and some pious women from Galilee, who know that your body is precious. Their hands represent the hands of all who never tire of serving you and making visible the love of which human beings are capable. It is this love that makes us hope in the possibility of a better world. We need only be willing to let ourselves be met by the grace that comes from you. In prayer, we entrust to your Father, in a particular way, all prison guards and all those who work in various capacities in prisons.

Let us pray.

O God, eternal light and endless day, fill with your blessings those who devote themselves to your praise and to the service of those who suffer in the countless places of human pain and sorrow. Through Christ our Lord. Amen.

About Dialogue for Diversity and the Jesuit Centre for Faith and Justice

Dialogue for Diversity

Dialogue for Diversity was set up by Jesuits in Northern Ireland in 2009 to develop more respect and esteem for all groups in society, especially the marginalized. We work with people from all faith backgrounds and none. We focus on prisoners, peace-making, restoring the planet, community development and Catholic Church reform. Influenced by the conflict in Northern Ireland and its aftermath, we honour and value diversity, working with those on the edge of society and opposing sectarianism, racism and all forms of prejudice.

Jesuit Centre for Faith and Justice

The Jesuit Centre for Faith and Justice is an agency of the Irish Jesuit Province, dedicated to undertaking social analysis and theological reflection in relation to issues of social justice, including housing and homelessness, penal policy, environmental justice, and economic ethics. The Centre emerged from the work of a small group of Jesuits who were living and working in Ballymun in the late 1970s and has consistently sought to promote justice for all through social analysis, theological reflection, action, education, and advocacy. Twice a year we publish a journal of social analysis called *Working Notes*. Subscription is free. Information about the Centre and subscriptions to the journal can be found at: https://www.jcfj.ie/.

All proceeds from the sale of this book will go to Dialogue for Diversity and the Jesuit Centre for Faith and Justice.

Dialogue for Diversity